THEotherAMERICA

BATTERED Women

These and other titles are included in *The Other America* series:

THEotherAMERICA

BATTERED Women

by
Gail B. Stewart

Photographs by
Natasha Frost

Lucent Books, P.O. Box 289011, San Diego, CA 92198-9011

Cover design: Carl Franzen

Library of Congress Cataloging-in-Publication Data

Stewart, Gail, 1949-
    Battered women / by Gail B. Stewart ; photographs by Natasha Frost.
      p. cm. — (The other America)
    Includes bibliographical references and index.
    Summary: Following a factual introduction, four women of different ages and backgrounds who are now or have recently been battered tell their own stories in their own words.
    ISBN 1-56006-341-6 (alk. paper)
    1. Abused women—United States—Juvenile literature. 2. Abused wives—United States—Juvenile literature. 3. Family violence—United States—Juvenile literature. [1. Abused women. 2. Family violence.] I. Frost, Natasha, ill. II. Title. III. Series: Stewart, Gail, 1949– Other America.
   HV6626.2.S75   1997
   362.82′92′0973—dc20   96–32583
                                                CIP
                                                AC

Printed in the U.S.A.
Copyright © 1997 by Lucent Books, Inc.
P.O. Box 289011, San Diego, CA 92198-9011

Contents

Foreword

O, YES,
I SAY IT PLAIN,
AMERICA NEVER WAS AMERICA TO ME.
AND YET I SWEAR THIS OATH—
AMERICA WILL BE!
LANGSTON HUGHES

Perhaps more than any other nation in the world, the United States represents an ideal to many people. The ideal of equality—of opportunity, of legal rights, of protection against discrimination and oppression. To a certain extent, this image has proven accurate. But beneath this ideal lies a less idealistic fact—many segments of our society do not feel included in this vision of America.

They are the outsiders—the homeless, the elderly, people with AIDS, teenage mothers, gang members, prisoners, and countless others. When politicians and the media discuss society's ills, the members of these groups are defined as what's wrong with America; they are the people who need fixing, who need help, or increasingly, who need to take more responsibility. And as these people become society's fix-it problem, they lose all identity as individuals and become part of an anonymous group. In the media and in our minds these groups are identified by condition—a disease, crime, morality, poverty. Their condition becomes their identity, and once this occurs, in the eyes of society, they lose their humanity.

The Other America series reveals the members of these groups as individuals. Through in-depth interviews, each person tells his or her unique story. At times these stories are painful, revealing individuals who are struggling to maintain their integrity, their humanity, their lives, in the face of fear, loss, and economic and spiritual hardship. At other times, their tales are exasperating, demonstrating a litany of poor choices, shortsighted thinking, and self-gratification. Nevertheless, their identities remain distinct, their personalities diverse.

As we listen to the people of *The Other America* series describe their experiences they cease to be stereotypically defined and become tangible, individual. In the process, we may begin to understand more profoundly and think more critically about society's problems. When politicians debate, for example, whether the homeless problem is due to a poor economy or lack of initiative, it will help to read the words of the homeless. Perhaps then we can see the issue more clearly. The family who finds itself temporarily homeless because it has always been one paycheck from poverty is not the same as the mother of six who has been chronically chemically dependent. These people's circumstances are not all of one kind, and perhaps we, after all, are not so very different from them. Before we can act to solve the problems of the Other America, we must be willing to look down their path, to see their faces. And perhaps in doing so, we may find a piece of ourselves as well.

Introduction

Nina could speak volumes about what it is like to be a woman in an abusive relationship. Not only is she a formerly battered woman, finally free of the husband who beat and raped her throughout a four-year marriage, but she is currently the director of a battered women's shelter in a suburb of Chicago. She says that the number of women and children who have been using her shelter has ballooned in the last two years.

"It's both good and bad," she says. "On the one hand, you might be glad that these women have the guts to leave their situations—at least for a little while. But on the other hand, it also indicates that there are more of these abusive relationships happening today than before. It scares me."

STAGGERING STATISTICS

Nina's suspicions about the growing number of battered women at her shelter are seconded by other shelters around the United States. Figures indicate that there were fifteen million women beaten or otherwise abused in 1995; that's approximately one every fifteen seconds. The FBI states that in the United States today it is far more likely for a woman to be raped or assaulted in her own home by a spouse or boyfriend than by a stranger on the street.

"There are fourteen hundred women killed by those abusive spouses or boyfriends each year," says Nina, "and numbers like these can't be ignored. I mean, we carry ourselves like we were the most informed, the most progressive society on earth. But we aren't so superior, not when you hear this stuff. It's a national disgrace, that's what it is!"

Battering is a term used to mean the abuse of one person in a relationship by another. While it is certainly true that men, also, are battered by their spouses and that gay or lesbian people are battered by their partners, the overwhelming majority of adult battering victims are women.

"It's also important to understand the many ways in which women are battered," says a counselor who works frequently with both batterers and their victims. "A lot of it is physical—slapping, punching, kicking. We see women with broken bones from being thrown down stairs, with black eyes and broken noses, and with more critical injuries from gunshots and knives. It is easy to see in cases such as these the total need for control batterers have. And since men are usually stronger than women, it is not so difficult for them to use physical violence to control."

However, this counselor stresses that there are other ways of battering that are just as hurtful. Sexual abuse is common, raping or forcing their wives or girlfriends to perform degrading or painful sexual acts. Verbal abuse is a powerful tool, too, and one that is commonly used. In fact, all of the women interviewed in this book were repeatedly called names, such as whore and slut. Lisa, one of the women, told her abusive boyfriend that if he didn't stop his abuse, she would leave. His reaction was to tell her over and over that she was ugly and that no one would want her.

"Man, he did a real number on me," she admits. "I mean, if somebody tells you you're fat, or ugly, or your nose is too big—if they tell you that often enough, you start to believe it, you know?"

NOTHING NEW ABOUT BATTERED WOMEN

Although the statistics today show that more women are being abused, to assume that the problem is new would be wrong. Men have used intimidation and violence to control their wives for centuries. Even the Bible contains anecdotes that not only tolerate but encourage men's domination and control over women.

Wife beating was common in England during the Middle Ages and came to America with the colonists. One device used in colonial America was the scold's bridle, which a husband might use on his wife if she was outspoken or complained. The bridle was a sort of cage, which fit over the woman's head. When the door was closed on the cage, metal spikes would be embedded in the woman's tongue, teaching her a painful lesson.

Such abuse of women by their husbands was sanctioned by law, too. Since wives, like cattle and other livestock, were considered property in England and in Europe, it was perfectly permissible for men to beat their wives, if only to keep them in line. In fact, one often cited law of 1768 in England—which had heavy influence on American laws, as well—permitted the beating of a woman by her husband with a stick, as long as the stick was no thicker than his thumb. The common phrase "rule of thumb" comes from that law.

As time progressed, such laws began to disappear from the books. However, it was not until 1871 that Massachusetts and Alabama voted to declare wife beating illegal. But even though battering is now illegal, it is amazingly common in America today.

WHO BATTERS?

There is no easy way to spot a batterer—at least not on the surface. He may be Native American, white, Latino, or African-American. He may be poor, wealthy, or somewhere in between. He may be a city dweller or a suburbanite, or he may live on a farm. He may be loud and aggressive; he may be quiet and reserved.

"People are truly surprised when we tell them that there's no way to spot a batterer, at least until you know him," says a counselor at a women's shelter in St. Paul, Minnesota. "I think the notion that they're all poor men of color—as many assume that their victims are—comes from the fact that that's who we most often see. The poor are more likely to call for police, to use shelters, to get into the system. But don't think that there aren't batterers who are middle- or upper-class white men, too."

A woman named Marcie agrees. Her husband is a loan officer at a large suburban bank, a well-known figure in the community in which they live.

"He's funny, engaging, the life of every party," she says. "Until we go home. Then he feels the need to berate me and tell me how useless I am. I've been punched so many times over the years I've lost count. But I'd never turn him in, I'd never call the police, I'd never leave—and I'm not proud of that. But to do those things would hurt my children and embarrass me. Without Tom, I wouldn't have the nice house in the nice community. So I just feel ashamed, and I know I've let myself down."

Under the Surface

There are a number of behavioral traits that batterers are likely to share, says a recent study by the National Coalition Against Domestic Violence. They tend to be insecure, for example, and as a result may compensate by using drugs or alcohol. They are more likely than other men to have sudden fits of anger or rage.

They may experience strong feelings of jealousy when they see a wife or girlfriend talking to another man or even looking at another man. Megan, one of the young women interviewed in this book, saw that side of her boyfriend many times.

"One time we were at McDonald's and he beat up a guy so bad it put him in a coma. The reason, [he] said, was because the guy looked at me. Charlie [my boyfriend] asked me if I knew the guy, and I said no, because I didn't. That's all it took for Charlie to go after him. For nothing, just for nothing."

It was not long afterwards that her boyfriend switched the object of his rage from the boys who looked at or talked to Megan to Megan herself—something experienced by several of the women in this book.

Not Only One Victim

Battered women are victims, without doubt. However, they are often not the only victims in a battering relationship. Children, too, get hurt in such cases of domestic violence.

"Sometimes children, even very young ones, are beaten," says one domestic violence worker. "They may be trying to protect their mother by stepping between their parents during an attack, or they may simply be standing nearby, watching. The batterer may decide to hurt them as a way of hurting their mother. But they frequently get beaten, too."

Ironically, she says, the children are one of the reasons often given by battered women when asked why they continue to stay with an abusive spouse:

"A woman will often say, 'I need to keep our marriage going, so the kids have a father.' But when you read the statistics, they say the opposite. For instance, kids who haven't even been beaten but have just been witnesses to their father's battering their mother— they are scarred. They are far more likely to have drug or alcohol abuse problems later on. They often grow up nervous and fearful.

11

Many become batterers themselves down the line. And I know that almost 80 percent of kids in institutional settings—jails, detox centers, shelters, and so on—80 percent are kids who watched their mothers getting beat up on a regular basis. Don't tell me these kids benefit from these mothers trying to keep the marriage alive."

WHY DOESN'T SHE JUST LEAVE?

One of the most common questions asked about the domestic violence issue is why a woman stays with someone who abuses her. Why would anyone put herself—and her children—in such danger?

Answers are diverse, and most battered women claim that a person would need to experience the same situation to understand.

Nina, the director of the battered women's shelter, says, "They are not strong. All they have to do is take a look at their situation and realize they have very little power. They've been told how worthless they are, and they've come to believe it. Think about the guts it takes to leave a man like that, pack up the kids and leave. That's a mountain bigger than most of them could imagine climbing.

"And the financial consequences are scary, too, especially in cases where the woman depends on the man to bring home a paycheck. How will they survive? And since they are the ones who are leaving, what will they do for a home? What can they afford? How can she keep feeding those kids, buying them clothes and everything else, if she's living in poverty?"

Many battered women say that they suffer from feelings of isolation, being completely cut off from family and friends or anyone else whom they might normally be able to confide in. In fact, isolating his wife or girlfriend from her friends or family is a very common tactic of a batterer.

"I was told I couldn't go outside any more," says one formerly battered woman. "He told me I couldn't see my friends and I couldn't even use the phone. I was so tired of being alone all day, being cut off from everyone. I needed to talk, needed to cry on my sister's shoulder."

NOT JUST BY ACCIDENT

Even though it is true that most battered women say they are shocked to find that their husband or boyfriend turns out to be violent, it is important to understand that battered women usually play a key role in allowing the violence to continue. Instead of leaving the instant the relationship turns violent, most women remain—for a number of reasons. Most, say social workers, lack the self-esteem it takes to convince themselves that they deserve something better.

"I grew up in a nice home, but my mom and us kids were pretty much told what to do," says Yvonne. "My dad was the boss, and we all knew it. I sort of grew up thinking that was pretty normal, for the man to tell you what's okay and what's not. I mean, my mom did it. It never dawned on her to question the way things were, I think. And when Terry [my boyfriend] started beating me up—I mean, it came up so gradually, from a push, to a little slap, to worse—it didn't seem shocking. At least not until I looked at the whole pattern, years afterwards."

Others come from families where there were no opportunities for them to be strong or successful.

"Some never did well in school or never finished," says Nina. "Lots had babies before they themselves were grown. Lots of them never had anybody in their lives to urge them on, to make sure they had goals and were supportive when these girls worked to-wards those goals."

Some women who remain with batterers are like Dina, afraid for their lives and the lives of their children, if they were to leave.

"I knew what Ben was capable of," she says. "He'd told me over and over that if I left or if I called the cops, he'd kill me. I believed him. The way I figured, there was no shelter in this city that could keep that man from getting his hands on me when he was mad like that."

Another commonly shared feeling among many women who stay with men who abuse them is the hope that those men will change. They convince themselves that if they are patient enough, or kind enough, the battering will stop.

"I love him," says Carmen, a young woman interviewed here. "He was only a batterer sometimes, not even 5 percent of the time, I bet. Most of the time he was good and sweet and generous. I just knew that eventually he'd learn how to solve his problem. Then we'd be perfect."

"I didn't leave because I knew he'd get better; he was just going through hard times," says one young woman. "I'd feel so guilty, too, because I'd talked myself into feeling like it was my fault, like

I'd done something to provoke him, you know? My fault that he raped me, my fault that he put a gun to my chest, my fault that he called me horrible names. I remember apologizing to *him* after episodes like that!"

Unfortunately, say domestic violence experts, such unfailing devotion is almost never successful. A woman who believes that love will correct her situation is only fooling herself.

THE STORIES OF FOUR WOMEN

In this book, *The Other America: Battered Women*, readers are introduced to four women who are now, or have recently been, battered. Their ages vary, as do their backgrounds. Each of the women tells her own story, in her own words.

Megan, an attractive twenty-year-old from a middle-class suburb, was battered for more than two years by her boyfriend. It took a rape at gunpoint to convince her that there was no future with him.

Carmen, a woman from Chicago, insists that she still loves the boyfriend who broke her eardrum by punching her in the side of the head. She is certain that people can change, and that even though the two are no longer together—Rick is in prison for his abuse of another girlfriend—they could reunite eventually.

Lisa, a mother of four who can recite lists of people in her family who have been abused or murdered, is recently separated from her abusive boyfriend. She knows she is through with him, although she admits that since the abuse, she herself has become more violent—especially toward boyfriends.

Finally, there is Mary, the mother of seven children. She beams with pride when she tells of how she finally fought back when her husband beat her. "That was a turning point," she says, "and I decided I wasn't going to let no man do that to me anymore."

Megan

"I WAS OPTIMISTIC. I THOUGHT IF
I TRIED HARD ENOUGH, THINGS
WOULD WORK OUT. WE MOVED IN
TOGETHER, AND I WAS HOPING
THAT MY OPTIMISM WOULD PAY
OFF. I WANTED TO BE RIGHT. I
WANTED TO BELIEVE THAT I WAS
CAPABLE OF CHANGING HIM."

The attractive home is on a quiet street in a suburb of the city.
The oak and maple trees are large, the lawns well tended. In this
home, owned by Megan's mother, family pictures and plants are
carefully placed throughout the living room, and an old red glass
candy dish sits on a table, an heirloom from Megan's great-aunt,
who recently died.

Megan seems so comfortable, so self-assured, it is difficult to
believe that she is a survivor of a relationship in which she was
almost murdered. The pretty twenty-year-old sits quietly on a
chair, hands folded on her lap.

"I sometimes talk to schools or other organizations about battered women," she says. "And I *always* get funny looks from
people when I tell them my story. It's as if they are surprised that
I'm white, or young. It is really sad that in our supposedly well-
informed society, with all the articles and television programs
about this subject, people still are carrying around stereotypes
of battered women.

"They think we're all minorities or poor, or we're chemically
dependent—either on crack or alcohol. One woman insisted to
me that she thought battered women were all fat and ugly and

therefore had no self-esteem. She thought that we allowed men to treat us so horribly because we were desperate to hold on to a man!"

She shakes her head in amazement.

"It's really something. I'm glad I'm out there talking about battered women, because I sure don't fit the stereotype. I'm middle-class, suburban, white, and not bad looking. I went to a nice little Catholic high school and got good grades, at least part of the time. I am not, nor was I ever, chemically dependent. I don't think I have a big problem with my self-confidence, but I'll be the first to admit that I've really changed in the last couple of years."

A CONTROLLING FATHER

Megan says that she can't complain about her upbringing, because her parents both loved her and were able to provide for their five children. However, her parents were not happy together, and Megan has vivid memories of her father controlling her mother. She admits that her reaction to her own abuse at the hand of her boyfriend might well have been affected by watching the way her father treated her mother.

"That was the way my father was," she shrugs. "He was always demeaning her—putting her down for the things she said or for what she did. If I asked to do something with friends, and I got permission from my mom, my dad would find out and yell at her for being too soft, too easy on me. When Dad talked, everybody listened; no one argued. Mom would just be quiet.

"That didn't seem strange or necessarily wrong, either. I mean, we kids weren't used to anything else, so we just assumed that was pretty normal: the dad was the boss, and the mom really didn't have much of a say. In fact, it wasn't until I was fifteen and my parents separated that I got to know what a neat lady my mom was, so smart and funny."

Megan says that her father did occasionally get physical with her mother, although because she was the youngest in the family, she was not as aware of it as her older brothers and sisters were.

"I know he pushed her around a little bit when he was yelling," she says. "And I felt really bad when it happened, because I felt loyal to my mom. But you know, even a kid learns pretty young in a situation like that, that if you disrespect your dad by defending your mom, she'll end up paying the price. She'll get hurt worse.

Megan and her mother hang out on their back porch. "I don't think of her as my mom," says Megan, "I think of her as a best friend."

"It did get to where I started really resenting my dad, especially when he initiated their separation. He wanted it because he said he wanted a whole new life. But then I found out that his whole new life was a new girlfriend that he was living with. In other words, he didn't want any part of this life he'd had with us. So I guess you could say I had a grudge against him. You can forgive and forget with your parents when you know they're trying hard to take care of the family the best they can. But when you find out something like this, that he's chosen to leave the family, then you don't forgive so quickly."

When Megan entered high school, she left the circle of friends she'd known in public school. Her mother had decided she wanted Megan to attend a small private school in their neighborhood; she told Megan it would be the best thing for her.

"My grades weren't too good in eighth grade, and my mom wanted me to go to this Catholic high school close by. I didn't want to go at first, because I was worrying about fitting in and about how much I was going to miss my friends who were going on to the public high school. But it was my mom's decision; she's

Megan met her boyfriend Charlie during a stressful time in her life. She says she immediately bonded with Charlie, whose parents were also in the process of divorcing.

put my older brother through that school, and it worked out fine for him."

Megan worried all summer before her freshman year about fitting in at this new school.

"I thought it was going to be awful," she admits. "I figured the boys would be really stuck up, real preppy. And the girls would be real cliquish and obnoxious. But it really wasn't like that at all. The kids were almost all nice, and I had no trouble making friends.

"But in my sophomore year, things were getting worse at home. This was about the time my dad left, and it really bothered me. I was mad at everybody, I think. I didn't know what to do. Everything was sort of out of my control. I started doing some drugs, mostly pot. It was no problem getting them at school. I even started selling the drugs to make a little extra money. I wasn't addicted or anything, but it sure helped me to relax and think about something other than the mess at home with my family and how worried I was."

MEETING CHARLIE

Selling drugs was precisely how Megan met the boy who would turn out to be her abuser. He was smoking pot at a party, she says, and she happened to be selling.

"There were lots of kids there from my school," Megan explains, "as well as the public high school where my old friends went. I got to talking to this one guy who looked a little familiar, and it turned out that he'd been in my class in fourth grade or something. We got to talking, and he seemed really fun to be around.

"I didn't know him very well back in grade school. I *did* remember that he was one of those little boys who is always getting in trouble for fighting, for wrestling on the playground. It was no big deal, though, for lots of boys played rough together when they were young.

"But he sure had changed physically," she says with a smile. "I mean, he was so good-looking—really drop-dead gorgeous! About six-two, really tan, and bright blue eyes. He had dark hair and was very, very fit. He was homecoming king at his high school. He played every sport there was, and he ended up being captain of all of them, it seemed."

Megan says that they got to laughing and reminiscing about grade school. Charlie also confided that his parents were in the process of a very difficult divorce, and his home situation was awful, too.

"I told him about my parents, too, and that seemed to be a real bond between us, that we could really talk," she says. "So we started hanging out together, talking a lot on the phone. Eventually we got to be boyfriend and girlfriend, and he was my first serious boyfriend. I'd never had sex or anything, I wasn't planning on starting sex at this point, either, but Charlie was the only one I'd ever thought about it with.

"Things just seemed to be going right at that point. I loved school; my grades were up; I wasn't doing the drugs anymore. I was happy—I guess it was as simple as that! I had friends, and I had a boyfriend. My mom wasn't crazy about him, because she remembered his name as one of the kids that roughhoused a lot in grade school, but she didn't make an issue out of it. It just seemed, at that point, that Charlie and I had a really good shot at a bright future together."

LITTLE SIGNALS

By junior year, however, there were little signals that Charlie was having trouble. He was having problems in school, and by the end of his junior year, Charlie had dropped out.

"He'd never been good at taking orders or obeying his teachers," she says. "He hated the vice-principal at his school. Charlie even told him to screw off one time. He loved getting into fights; he thought it was just a riot.

"That was when I started making excuses for Charlie. When I heard about the fighting in school and the rudeness to the vice-principal, I chalked it up to his being upset over his parents' divorce. His father had been married three times. Charlie hadn't even seen his real mother since he was nine. I figured that *had* to have an effect on him. After all, he just has a temper, and a temper wasn't unusual. And I told Charlie it was no big deal, that that vice-principal didn't understand him, that there was a personality clash. I urged Charlie not to give up, that he should just get his GED and that would be as good as a diploma."

Charlie got a job north of the city, working the late shift at an all-night gas station. Because he had no car, Megan took it upon herself to help him out by driving him home each morning.

"I'd get up at 4," she says, remembering. "I'd pick him up, take him home, and then rush home and take a shower before going off to school. Sometimes we'd sit and talk after work, and I'd really have to hurry. Lots of times I didn't make it to school until late.

"I don't know even now why I did that. It was a real inconvenience. It's certainly not because I enjoy getting up that early, that's for sure! But I thought it would be something I could do to make him happy. See, he never really seemed happy then, always kind of lost. I felt sorry for him, having to feel that way all the time."

NAME-CALLING AND FIGHTING

As the weeks and months went by, Megan says, Charlie's unhappiness began erupting into fits of anger, often directed at her.

"He'd get in a bad mood and then tell me to shut up when I was talking," says Megan. "I hadn't been arguing with him, or trying to tell him what to do, just normal conversation. And he started accusing me of things he'd never even hinted at before, like being unfaithful to him. He'd call me names like bitch and whore on a daily basis.

"But I told Charlie that I had no other boyfriends. I mean, I had lots of friends at school, and some of them were boys. But none were boyfriends. I told him that he was my only boyfriend, but he'd accuse me of sleeping with any boy I'd mentioned as a friend. Maybe to Charlie, because I don't think he'd ever had a girl for a friend, he couldn't understand the idea that you could be friends with someone of the opposite sex without sleeping together. I don't know."

Didn't she see this excessive, possessive jealousy as a warning sign? Megan shrugs.

"If you mean, did I think to myself, this is a dangerous guy who is going to eventually batter me, then, no. I figured he was going through hard times and that he was overstating the jealousy he felt. I mean, he didn't go to my school, he didn't see me with these friends—he just didn't understand how harmless these friendships were. I knew he was overreacting, but I just told myself that he was jealous because he cared about me. Of course, today I can look back and know that isn't so, but then it was an easy answer to give myself."

But Charlie's anger and frustration seemed to be getting worse. He began to get in serious fights on a regular basis, fights that Megan used to tell herself were because of his drinking. But she now knows better.

"It wasn't just the drinking," she says, "it was him. He couldn't control his temper, and he came close to killing someone. I mean, there were the fights he'd get into at parties, stuff like that. But one time we were at McDonald's and he beat up a guy so bad it put him in a coma. The reason, Charlie said, was because the guy looked at me. Charlie asked me if I knew the guy, and I said no, because I didn't. That's all it took for Charlie to go after him. For nothing, just for nothing."

After the incident at McDonald's, Charlie's father kicked him out of the house. In what proved to be a very unwise move, Megan begged her mother to allow Charlie to live with them.

THE FIRST TIME

Megan's mother was dubious about letting Charlie stay with them, even though Megan had kept the stories of Charlie's fighting and drinking to herself. Eventually she relented, voicing some of the same thoughts that Megan was feeling: that Charlie needed a mother figure in his life, someone who could be understanding as well as firm. And as if to prove her analysis, Megan's mother made Charlie promise that he would go to school and get a part-time job.

"He didn't, though," admits Megan. "He wasn't working on his GED; he'd quit his job. What he *would* do was get up with me in the mornings and drive me to school in my car. Then he'd take my car and go off with his friends all day, smoking pot and drinking. Then in the afternoons he'd come back and bring me home from school.

"It made me mad, because I was a senior then, and seniors were allowed to go off campus for lunch. But with no car, I was stuck. And lots of times he was late in picking me up after school. But I went along with it."

The physical abuse began during the time Charlie was living in Megan's home. Charlie had been taking acid that day, and he was in the mood to be alone.

"But I was bored," Megan says, "and I wanted to do something. I got him to come upstairs to my room and play backgammon with me. Well, anyway, I won the game, and it made me really happy. I was getting silly, and I stood up and danced around, celebrating.

"It happened so fast, I didn't even see it coming. Charlie stood up and picked me up and threw me across the room. He started breaking everything in the room: stuff on my desk, off my night-stand, everything. He was punching things, like glass pictures and mirrors, and there was blood all over the room."

TO THE HOSPITAL

Charlie grabbed Megan again and pushed her head so hard against the wall that her head actually went *through* the wall. Her mother heard the noise and came running up the stairs. Megan continues the story:

"She grabbed Charlie's arms and said, 'What are you doing to my daughter?' He didn't even say anything, just pushed her, too.

She went flying into the hallway and broke four of her ribs. She got up, though, and went to call the police.

"They came and took Charlie away. They asked me over and over if I was okay, because I looked so bad. I told them I was fine. There was blood all over me, but I didn't know it was mine until we sat down and the paramedics were looking at my mom and me. They found a big piece of glass that had embedded itself into my left foot and had cut the tendon on the bottom."

Megan shakes her head, knowing how foolish the next part sounds.

"When they took us to the hospital to do X rays on my mom and to stitch my foot up, you know what I was busy doing? Calling Charlie, making sure he was okay! I told him I wouldn't press charges, so he went back to his dad, who agreed to let him stay— at least temporarily.

"I was so worried that he'd get a record and it would be our fault. I'm thinking, 'He was angry, and I made him play backgammon when he didn't want to, and he's doing drugs. He's had a rough time, I should be more understanding.' I mean, I'm not

Megan says she doesn't fit the stereotype of a battered woman. "One woman . . . [I spoke with] thought battered women were all fat and ugly and therefore had no self-esteem," she remembers.

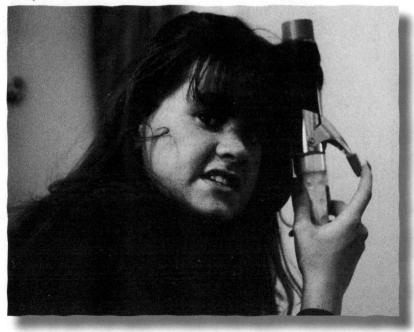

thinking about my mom or the fact that I'm on crutches because of my foot. I'm apologizing to *him*!"

MORE OF THE SAME

After that incident, Megan's mother banished Charlie from their home and urged her daughter not to get further involved with the boy. But Megan said that she couldn't just walk away.

"I knew more than ever how much he needed me," she says. "I mean, his reactions were so inappropriate, it didn't take much to see how troubled he was. But I felt like I was the one who could help him. I *wanted* to be the one. I told myself that he just needed to get that out of his system, all that built-up anger about things. I figured that it would blow over, and that would be that. So, when my birthday arrived, three days later, I wanted to spend it with him.

"My mom didn't want me to go, but she gave in after I promised her I'd be fine and that if he ever did anything like that to me again, I'd never see him again. And when I said it, I meant it—at least at the time."

Megan pets her cat Arnold. She says that despite her boyfriend Charlie's abuse, she felt sorry for him and decided to give him a second chance.

However, less than a minute after she hobbled up the steps of his father's house on her crutches, Charlie attacked her again.

"He came at me so fast I couldn't think," she remembers. "He threw me into the wall of his kitchen. I hit my head on the microwave and my bad foot on the refrigerator. His father grabbed me just as Charlie started tearing the house apart and calling me all the names I'd come to expect: bitch, whore, and anything else he could think of.

"As his father backed out of the driveway to drive me home, we could see through the window Charlie going crazy, throwing the VCR across the room, smashing the TV. What did I do on the way home? Apologize to his father, as though it were my fault. His dad asked me what that was all about, what set him off, and I told him Charlie was convinced I was cheating on him but that I wasn't. I remember him telling me that I should say yes, and satisfy him. I told him no, that I was going to get beat up either way, and I didn't want to make things worse by lying."

Charlie's father alerted the police to his son's outburst, and they arrested him. He was taken to a hospital for a psychiatric examination. Twenty minutes after he got there, he called Megan to say he was sorry. But again, it was Megan who did the apologizing.

"He said he could leave after his examination, but it would cost seventy-five dollars to get bailed out," she says. "I thought, Oh God, I've got to get him out of that place. I was imagining all kinds of crazy people walking around, and him not belonging there. So I called one of his friends to come stand outside my window, and I put the money in a shoe and tossed it out to him."

SECRECY AND LYING

Charlie was able to leave the hospital, but he spent the next few months in limbo. He had no job and nowhere to stay, since his father had forbidden him to come back home. For money he relied on Megan.

"I kept giving him money," she admits. "I mean, normally, I wouldn't have even had money to give him, but I'd just had my birthday, and I'd gotten some money. But it all went to Charlie. He used it for motel rooms, for food, and for drugs and liquor.

"I'd sneak around to see him. I had to sneak, since I'd promised my mom that I wouldn't see him. I just wanted to be with him, to help him. I couldn't help feeling that in a way it was my fault that he was in this position, although I know now that was far from the truth. I had to lie; I told my mom that I was spending the weekend with girlfriends from school, and she believed me.

"I was good at lying then," she says with a sad smile. "My mom trusted me. When I was on crutches, and everyone at school asked me what happened, I made up a really believable story about my mother dropping a glass in my room and how we thought we'd gotten all the pieces. But then I jumped off the waterbed and stepped right on a big chunk. Everybody bought it.

"The only person that didn't believe any of my lies was this teacher I had for child psychology. She was nice, and she kind of understood what we would be talking about, even when she didn't seem to be listening, you know? But she'd notice how I acted, how I'd be crying sometimes or looked like I had bruises.

"Especially hard was when we were on this unit about child abuse. I mean, it wasn't about battered women, but it was so close that it really bothered me, and she could sense that. I found out later that she had a hunch about what was going on with me all that time. She told me later that she prayed for me every night. I guess that's all she could do. I'd never talked to her when it was going on. I wish I had."

BUSTED, AND A PROPOSAL

It wasn't long before Charlie's temper, along with his drinking and drug use, got him in serious trouble. He got into a serious fight at a party and was arrested. Megan continues:

"He was sent away to a correctional facility for juveniles. I went with his dad every weekend to see him. It's funny—it was kind of cool in a way. Having a boyfriend who was in jail was kind of different; it sort of raised my status with some of the kids I knew. I mean, it wasn't as though he had murdered anyone. It was just for fighting. Lots of kids were really sympathetic. They said, 'That's too bad; the police always overreact'—stuff like that. They never knew the whole story, about his battering me."

Charlie was able to get released a month early because he'd agreed to go through rehabilitation for his drinking and drug use. About a week before he was scheduled to be released from rehab, Megan says, he proposed to her.

"He asked me to go find a place where we could start living together as soon as he got out," she remembers. "And at first, to be truthful, I had some real doubts. I didn't know he wanted to get married that soon. He explained that it wasn't that he was in a hurry to get married, but he thought we should live together to see if we were compatible.

"I ended up getting the basement of my great-aunt's house. She lived in a western suburb, a really beautiful area. She was skeptical about a boy and a girl living together. She asked me if it was okay with my mom. I kind of stretched the truth and told her that my mom thought it was time for me to get out on my own.

"If there was any doubt in her mind," Megan smiles sadly, "Charlie erased it. He was so charming to her, she just couldn't refuse. That's the part that never changed—he could be so nice when he wanted to be. No one would ever guess, looking at that handsome face, the kinds of things he was capable of."

"I'll Pray Every Day That You Come Out Alive"

One of the most difficult aspects of moving in with her great-aunt, Megan says, was telling her mother of her plans.

"I told her, and she cried," says Megan softly. "That wasn't like her at all. I told myself, 'Don't cry, Megan, because then she'll know that something is wrong.' I was worried—scared, in fact— that Charlie would hurt me again. And I didn't want her to worry about that or to know that I was even thinking about it.

"She told me, 'Have a nice life, Megan, because I can't deal with any of this at all. No matter what happens, though, I'll always be your mother, and I'll pray every day that you come out alive.'"

Megan says that she lied, telling her mother that Charlie had never actually slapped or punched her. But her mother shook her head and told her that she was just playing word games and was only fooling herself.

"She told me, 'Your father never actually slapped me or punched me in the beginning, either. But you'll be rationalizing your whole life—first, that he doesn't slap you. Then it will be, he doesn't punch you. And pretty soon it will be, he wouldn't kill me.'

"I told my mom, 'You don't know me, how it is for me. You're so much older that you don't have any idea of the kinds of things kids go through these days.' I was hoping that Charlie and I would start having a good life, in our own little space, and that

27

Megan frequently accepts speaking engagements at area schools. "Every time I share my story it gets a little easier, it gets a little lighter on my shoulders," she says.

things would work out. I know now how this sounds—as though I didn't have a clue. I mean, he's hitting me, doing all kinds of things to hurt me, so why was I moving in with him?

"It's that I was optimistic. I thought if I tried hard enough, things would work out. I didn't see it as Charlie needing to work hard or to change. And besides, to tell you the truth, the hitting didn't bother me even half as much as the name-calling. Being called bitch and whore was more damaging to me, more shocking than getting slapped around. So we moved in together, and I was hoping that my optimism would pay off. I wanted to be right.

I wanted to believe that I was capable of changing him. But when the hitting and the threats and the name-calling started coming full force after that, I remembered my mom's words in my head."

"I WAS THE ADULT IN THE RELATIONSHIP"

Megan insists that the first twenty days were nicer than she ever could have imagined. Spending time with Charlie and her great-aunt was fun, and the three of them got along well.

"My great-aunt would come downstairs and eat with us. I was really having fun cooking," she says. "I always had felt kind of sorry for her, because she ate such a bland diet—not for health reasons, but because she didn't want to go to a lot of trouble just for herself. But I made big dinners, desserts, salads, everything. The three of us would sit there each night like a happy little family. Her hearing and her eyesight were poor, but she really enjoyed our company.

"But after those first twenty days, he started going out to bars with his friends. At first I was pretty sure that he wasn't drinking, since he'd been so good after coming home from rehab. But then when he started coming home with the smell of beer on him, coming in at 4:30 in the morning, I knew he was sliding backwards.

"At first, he felt bad about it. I know he did," she insists. "He tried to hide that smell from me by throwing his clothes in the closet. But I told him that the smell came from the skin, so it didn't do any good to be sneaky hiding his clothes. He turned his face to the wall, and that time I could hear him crying softly."

Megan says that she began rationalizing again, excusing his behavior for a number of reasons.

"I thought, He's angry with me because I don't drink, I don't like to go to bars," she says. "I was the adult in the relationship, and he probably didn't like that. I told myself, 'Okay, he'll have one beer after work, and then he'll be fine.' But then it was two or three, and then a case, in addition to a couple of bottles of vodka.

"He got a job, though, at a little mini-mart. He worked the night shift and started stealing money out of the cash register. I found out about it and really got mad. I told him how dishonest it was and how mean it was to the old man who ran the store. I told Charlie that the guy had trusted him, had even told him what a good worker he was. The guy was eighty years old, I told Charlie. None of it was fair."

"I Had No Life"

Her protests accomplished nothing other than beatings. Megan looks ashamed as she admits that she even made excuses for Charlie's abusive behavior.

"I thought to myself, Gee, Megan, get off his case; he's probably having problems because he's drinking again. But the hitting and punching got worse and worse. I had black eyes, bumps, bruises all over my body. He'd hit me a lot in the back of the head, where nobody could see it. I could feel it, though, because I'd comb my hair and I would be in agony. Or I couldn't sleep on my back, because even the pillow made my head pound.

"He'd tell me not to tell anyone. He said that no one would believe me anyway. And so after a while, I just believed him. I wasn't going to school anymore, and I had stopped calling my friends. I didn't even answer the phone. No one saw my black eyes, since I

Megan likes to tell her story to show people that abuse can happen to anyone. "I'm young and white. I'm not one of the statistics."

didn't go to school, and I'd stopped going to work. My great-aunt couldn't see well enough to know, and once in a while when my mom would call and want to see me, I'd just tell her I was too busy with work, or something like that. And after a while, it was as if I had no life, other than being in that basement. I had no friends; I saw no one.

"If, by some miracle, I wanted to go out, to get together with someone—even my mom—he'd tell me he was going out, so I couldn't use the car. He'd tell me he really wanted me home when he came home, because he liked it when I was waiting for him. That part made me feel good, being needed like that. Of course, he'd never be home by ten, or by midnight, or even by two. I'd be stuck there, every time. It was a control thing, but I still kept assuring him that I loved him."

"THERE'S GOT TO BE SOMETHING WRONG WITH YOU"

The abuse was over nothing, Megan says. Charlie gave her one of her worst beatings because she'd ordered Chinese food that had peas, which he didn't like.

"I had been trying to make a nice romantic evening, trying to regain what we'd lost," she explains. "I had a little fire in the fireplace, and I'd gotten some beef lo mein, which he really likes. The lady at the carryout had given me the kind with peas, even though I had asked for without. And I thought about asking her to change the order, but I was in a hurry, and I thought, What the heck—he can pick the peas out, like I pick tomatoes out of stuff, you know?

"But when he came home and saw the dinner, he got irate. He knocked me down on the floor and started hitting me over and over with a broomstick. It wasn't so much that the abuse was getting worse, it was just that he was getting more creative about what he'd hurt me with. Brooms, sticks—even opening a door and pushing it back in my face—he always found a way to hurt me.

"I ended up doing a lot of crying, and he found that really strange. He said one time, 'You know, there's got to be something wrong with you. You cry too much. It isn't normal for a girl to cry this much, like you do.' I don't even know what he was thinking."

"I Was Crying So Hard I Couldn't Even Talk"

The relationship ended one night when a friend of Megan's named Marie came over unexpectedly. Marie hadn't seen Megan in a while and wanted her to come to a party with some of the kids from school. Megan was doubtful that Charlie would allow it, but the idea of seeing her friends again was tempting.

"Marie went home to change for the party, saying she would come back and get me in a little while," she says. "Charlie had been in the other room when Marie and I were talking, so he didn't know what was going on. He was getting ready to go out himself, and he told me that I couldn't go. Then he thought a minute and said that I could go if I'd have sex with him first.

"I was still a virgin—I really wanted to wait until we were married. So I told him no. But then he walked real fast into the bathroom, and came back with some kind of cord, like an old clothesline or something. He came back in, knocked me down, and tied up my feet and hands. I knew that he was going to rape me, I just knew. I tried talking to him, trying to distract him, but he wouldn't listen. He got a gun out of the drawer and raped me, holding the gun tight against my chest the whole time.

"It hurt so much. It was awful, I can't even explain how awful. The way he just stood up afterwards and got the car keys and just left me there, still tied up."

Megan says that Marie came back soon afterwards, and when she saw what Charlie had done to Megan, she was livid.

"She untied my wrists and was telling me how this had to stop, that no one should be living like this. I was crying so hard I couldn't even talk. But I wanted to leave; I wanted to go to the party. I just had to get out and do something normal, you know? Marie kept trying to make me promise never to come back to that apartment. She said my life was really in danger."

"He Had Taken Everything from Me"

Megan went to the party with her friends and soon realized that she was in worse shape than she had thought.

"I was around all of these kids, and they were, you know, just regular kids with regular lives. They were happy, having fun. And I looked at myself in the mirror, and I looked like hell. My eyes were so red and puffy from crying; my head was a mess of lumps.

And when I was reaching up to get something above the refrigerator, one of the guys noticed that I had a huge black-and-blue mark on my back.

"He asked me what that was from. I looked him in the eye and said, 'Charlie beats me.' And you know what his reaction was? He laughed! He didn't believe me at all, because I'd always had this reputation at school for being real independent, real tough. I mean, you just didn't mess with me or do anything to my friends, because I was really loyal. I don't mean kids were afraid of me—I had friends in every grade at school. But I was respected, you know?

"But he realized I was serious, the way I looked at him. He said, 'Megan, you wouldn't even let anyone tell you to shut up, let alone hurt you like that.' And I started crying. Marie came over, and showed them the black-and-blue marks on my legs and the rope burns on my wrists. The kids were horrified. They were all saying, 'Oh my God, Megan, you can come home to stay with me. I told them no, that I had to handle it, and I was going to start by taking control of my life. I knew I had to. He had taken everything from me—my car, my work, my school, and my friends. And now, my virginity. I felt like I had nothing."

MURDER THREATS AND GUNS

Charlie called the party as Megan was talking to her friends. He warned her that if she didn't come home immediately, he'd come over and crack her skull.

"I refused," says Megan. "I told him I wasn't ever coming home again, that he could have anything in the basement that he wanted. He got mad, told me that he was on his way over there to kill me, and that he was bringing one of his friends. I knew he wasn't kidding. I called the police, told them to get here as fast as they could. The party had changed from having fun and laughing to everyone sitting in the living room terrified.

"We heard him before we saw him. He raced up to the house, his car skidding to a stop. He had a gun and shot out all the windows. Whatever he and his friend didn't shoot at, they threw rocks at. There was glass everywhere. And they left, screeching off in the car before the police even arrived. I figured he was running back to our basement apartment, and I told the police when they came. They asked if I was willing to press charges, and I told them yes. I think even then, in the back of my mind, I was thinking that I could always change my mind."

Megan said she would go with the police back to her great-aunt's house. Knowing her mother was out of town, she called her father, even though her relationship with him since his leaving was rocky, at best. She asked him to come with her, for support.

"There were two ironic things that happened that night. The first was when my dad came to take me to the apartment. All the way over there, he was furious. He kept saying, 'Who would do things like that to a lady? How could he have done this?' I'm thinking to myself, You did—or at least you used to, but I didn't say it out loud. I figured that at least we were sort of getting along, and I didn't want to spoil it.

"The other irony was when we got to my great-aunt's and saw the destruction. He'd taken all my stuff and thrown it out on the lawn. Everything he could have smashed, he did. There was glass all over, from the photographs we'd had inside, pictures of us at prom, stuff like that. The only thing not broken was on our kitchen table—an empty bottle of vodka."

A NEW PROBLEM

Charlie was tried and convicted, although because he was not twenty-one, he was charged as a juvenile. He was sentenced to eight years and served only six months.

"Even so," she says, "he was completely amazed that I'd gone through with it. He had been looking at me during the trial, smiling and winking, like it was all a big joke. But when the verdict came down, he was shocked. He turned completely white. He never believed I would actually press charges; he was sure I'd chicken out at the last minute and change my mind."

However, even with Charlie in jail and threats of more abuse gone, there were some problems that lingered. Megan moved back with her mother and was trying to get her life back together, but she was stressed and unhappy.

"I was crying, getting mad at my mom over nothing at all," she says. "Then it came to me that I hadn't had my period for a long time. I hoped it was just the ordeal I'd been through, but I called one of my sisters and asked her to help me do a pregnancy test. It came out positive, and I was so sad, so furious, I didn't know how to react. I'd had sex only once, and it was a rape, at that. One time, and I was pregnant with the child of a guy I never wanted to see again."

THE SOLUTION THAT SEEMED BEST

"I didn't know what to do. I didn't want to be a mom yet. But then, I was responsible for that baby. I knew I *could* raise a child on my own. After all, my mom had done it. But then I started thinking about all the different options, and my head was swimming with all kinds of questions.

"I had a restraining order against Charlie, so that even when he got out of jail, he couldn't see me. I asked the judge if I could extend that to cover the baby, too. I knew I wanted to keep that child from Charlie, and who knew what he'd do? But the judge said no, that restraining orders were made when someone had threatened someone's life, and that Charlie had never threatened the baby. It was so stupid. I told the judge that's because there had never *been* any baby! But no was the answer.

"I thought about putting the baby up for adoption, giving that baby a life and giving it away, but ruled that out immediately. I

Megan helps her five-year-old niece, Felicia, dig through an Easter basket. Megan enjoys frequently baby-sitting her niece and nephew.

had given up drugs and drinking long before, but who knows if they would affect the baby? Were they still in my system? And Charlie's drug and alcohol abuse—certainly all of that would have an effect on the baby's health. I'd never give up a retarded baby for adoption. I couldn't do that.

"I decided to abort, although I'd never have thought I could do that. I'd always thought of that as wrong, at least for me. But to worry about the baby's health, and to be helpless to keep Charlie from hurting it or even trying to get visitation and poisoning that baby's mind somehow with all his stupid thoughts—I couldn't do anything else.

"I never regretted it. I went with my mom to the clinic and looked around at all these couples with wedding rings on. It was weird. I don't know how all of those people justified it, but that wasn't my problem. I knew it was right for me."

A NEW LIFE

In the months since then, Megan has begun a new life. She finished her high school degree, much to the delight of her parents.

"I was thinking at graduation that less than a year ago, I was being abused, battered, raped, and I got pregnant and had an abortion. Things can change so fast," she says evenly.

"I have enlisted in the air force, too. My brother had been in, and he liked it a lot. It's something I've always thought about doing, and I have decided to do it. I admit, I'm not sure exactly what I'll do there. Maybe helicopters. But if I don't get to do that, I'll make the best of it. If I have to be a garbage collector on the base, I'll be the best garbage collector. I want to be on my own, learn some new things, see places I've never seen.

"I have a boyfriend, but not a real serious relationship at all. I feel very protective of myself, and I'm not going to get into anything I can't handle. I've learned I have no tolerance for rudeness on the part of guys or any little hint of jealousy. I know better now, and it feels good to be so strong inside."

Has she seen Charlie at all since he's gotten out of jail? Megan shakes her head.

"He still lives around here; I know that much. Friends have told me they've seen him. But I have no interest in ever seeing him again, because he's worthless. I did see him from a distance, backing his car out of a store parking lot once.

Megan and her new boyfriend David enjoy the spring weather. "I keep thinking that he is going to be rude, be like all the other guys, but he is really different," says Megan.

"You know another irony? I was giving a talk once in a high school. I was describing what happened to me and the mistakes I'd made in that relationship. I used Charlie's name, but not his last name or anything. Anyway, this girl came up afterwards to talk to me. She told me that her boyfriend was named Charlie, too, and that from the description I gave of him—handsome, dark-haired, blue eyes—they sounded a lot alike, at least physically.

"But she said, 'My Charlie's got a temper, too, but nothing like your Charlie. I mean, he's pushed me around but never has punched me or anything like that.' I'm listening to her, and little alarm bells are going off in my head. She's talking about her broken collarbone, says he pushed her into a wall.

"I said, 'His last name doesn't happen to be ———, does it?' She looked at me, really surprised, and nodded her head yes. I got tears in my eyes. I told her that the best thing she could ever do was to get out of the relationship, walk away before she got killed someday."

Megan covers her eyes, remembering.

"I was listening to her rationalize his abuse, his battering. Saying it wasn't so bad. It really hit me then. God, she sounded just like me!"

Carmen

**"I FIGURED HIS BEING JEALOUS
JUST PROVED HOW MUCH I MEANT
TO HIM. I WISH HE'D SHOWN IT IN
A DIFFERENT WAY. AND NOW I
KNOW THAT WHAT HE WAS
SHOWING HAD NOTHING TO DO
WITH LOVE. BUT TO ME, AL-
THOUGH IT HURT ME, HURT MY
FEELINGS, I DIDN'T LEAVE HIM."**

Carmen is in her mid-twenties. She and her two sons live just
north of the city in a homeless shelter. This afternoon she is outside, enjoying the warm sun as she watches her children play. She
is an attractive woman, but a close look shows that she has bruises
on her face, particularly around her right eye, and her hand has a
dangerous-looking wound that appears to be the result of a bite.

"I have no plans to stay here, that's for sure," she says in a shy,
soft voice. "I came here after spending two months in a shelter for
battered women, and that was as long as they'd keep me. But me
and my boys are going to find a place where we can be on our
own. This is all real temporary."

Carmen calls to her two sons—Parris, age six, and Darrian, age
four. They walk slowly from the jungle gym where they have been
playing. Parris scowls, seeing that his mother is not alone. Darrian
comes up to Carmen and jumps in her arms.

"Hi, Mama," he says. "You okay?"

Carmen smiles and nods, unconsciously rubbing the bite on
her hand.

"You guys play nice over there, hear me? Parris, you watch your brother while I talk for a minute. I'll come push you on the swings later."

Parris, his face expressionless, gives a small nod and walks back towards the playground. Carmen sighs.

"This has been so hard on them," she says quietly.

GROWING UP IN CHICAGO

Carmen is a transplant from Chicago, lured north by the prospects of a better life.

"I grew up in my grandfather's house," she says. "My mother passed when I was thirteen; she was only twenty-nine. It was a drug overdose—heroin, I think. She'd shoot drugs then, but she hadn't been doing that when I was little. She was into it when I was twelve and thirteen, though. I never knew my father.

"I liked living with my grandfather. He was a good man—still is today. Retired from the post office, real good provider. A Christian man, you know? In fact, I have two other kids, older than Parris and Darrian, and they're living back there with him. They love him. He's raised them since they were babies."

The reason she is not raising those children, Carmen explains, is that she had them when she was a teenager, and she admits she knew nothing about being a mother.

"I was too young, too interested in running around with my friends," she says. "I was having troubles dealing with my mother's death; I was wild. Things weren't right, and my grandfather and me, we both knew that I wasn't doing right by those children. One time I got into some trouble and stayed gone for two weeks. My grandfather called children's services, told them I wasn't living up to my responsibilities as a mother. So he got custody of my kids. Under this agreement I wasn't supposed to live there no more, but I visited. The only way I could get them back was to go to court and prove that I was ready to be a good mother to those kids."

"LEAVING WOULD BE A GOOD IDEA"

For a while Carmen moved in with her girlfriend and her mother, in a low-income housing project on the north side of the city. She learned to be more independent, she says, but at the same time enjoyed having a mother around, even if it wasn't her own.

"After a while they moved from the projects," she says, "and I wanted to be on my own. I got an apartment—and I mean a *nice* apartment—on South Shore Drive. There were nice people living there, and wealthy people, too. It wasn't no run-down place; it was something. The reason I could get in there was that they had a few units in that building set aside for Section 8 [low-income] housing. And my aunt knew the manager of the building, so she got me in there.

"I had had Parris by then and was pregnant with Darrian. And for a while it was great, nicer than any place I'd ever had. But then Darrian's father started coming around late at night, yelling outside my window. I didn't want nothing to do with him. I'd told him that before. He was going one way, with his drugs and stuff, and I was trying to go the other way, the right way. So I didn't want him around at all.

"But he kept it up, coming around yelling up at me to come down or to let him in. I told him to stop it. I even called the police, and they'd come and take him away. But he'd come back another time, and he'd do the same thing. So pretty soon I started getting warnings from the manager that the other residents were complaining about all his noise. I didn't blame them for complaining. It bothered me, too. I told him to stop it, but he didn't, and eventually I got kicked out of there."

Carmen ended up in a Salvation Army shelter not long after that. At the shelter she met a girl named Michelle, who told her that she planned to leave Chicago. She urged Carmen to do the same. Life would be better up north, Michelle promised, and cities up there were more supportive of women trying to raise their kids alone.

"She talked me into it," says Carmen. "I thought to myself, leaving would be a good idea. There wasn't anything holding me there, except my older kids, and I wasn't raising them anyway. Me and my two boys, we just got on the bus and left. Michelle and her four kids did, too.

"I don't mean it wasn't hard to leave," says Carmen quickly, her eyes filling with tears. "My kids are nine and ten, the ones at my grandfather's, and they miss me. I miss them, too, even though I know they're happy where they are. But being so far from there, being in a different state—that's a lot different from being just on the other side of the city, you know?"

40

Carmen and her children left Chicago hoping to make a fresh start in a new city.

MEETING RICK

Carmen met Rick when she arrived in Minneapolis, within minutes of getting off the bus.

"[The children and I] went to the welfare office so that we could get some immediate help, like emergency housing," she explains. "We didn't have anything when we got there, just the clothes or whatever that we'd packed. I decided I'd get on welfare for a short time, but I had no interest in any long-term thing. I mean, that's a dead end, and I know it. But like I said, I wanted to start a new life, get me a job, get these boys in school. And since we had no one, nowhere to live, I had to get started somewhere.

"Rick had gotten here just the day before, from Gary, Indiana— said he had 'family troubles,' and he was going to start over here. He was getting a voucher for some emergency housing, just like we were. I'll tell you, he was a handsome man. He was black but had these bright green eyes. It really made people notice him quick. He was thin, but he had some muscle on him. A fine-looking man.

"Even though I noticed that right off, I acted like I didn't, though." She laughs. "I mean, I know that it's the person inside that's important. Later, when we were living together, he'd always remind me about that, saying, 'You didn't even act like I was good-looking, and that's one of the things I liked about you.'"

Carmen remembers that both she and Michelle liked Rick, for he seemed friendly and sociable and extremely fond of the children.

"We ended up going to the same shelter that night," Carmen says. "It was called the Drake, and it wasn't much of a place. The women and children didn't usually stay there. They usually gave them rooms in the shelter across the street, but they were all full up. I remember that the food was the worst thing; some people said it was worse than jail slop. For breakfast we had grits, but they were pink! It tasted old and kind of sour. My kids wouldn't eat it; they just called it 'the pink stuff.' And the meat at dinner? Man, that was mystery food, that's what it was. No one had a clue what kind of meat that was."

"ALMOST LIKE A FAMILY"

"But it was nice for us during the day, having Rick to hang around. We had all kinds of errands, you know—signing up for different programs, getting registered, filling out forms. And when we'd get done with that for the day, we'd go to the park across the street and hang out.

Carmen says that as the days went on, she and Rick started getting closer and began seeing each other as more than just friends.

"We made kind of an agreement while we were waiting for our apartments to come through," she says. "We promised that we'd live together, that if he got an apartment first, I'd go with him. If I

42

got mine first, he'd come live with me and the boys. I know now that that was my biggest mistake, getting so closely involved with him right off. I should have taken the time to get to know him. But then, it seemed right.

"As it turned out, I got assigned my apartment first, so Rick and me and the kids moved in. It was over on the north side, and it wasn't too bad a place. I was really excited, although maybe that sounds kind of silly now. But it felt like we were almost like a family, him being so good with the kids and all."

She shakes her head, remembering those times.

"He was so generous," she says. "He liked those kids a lot, and he'd buy them things all the time. He was always willing to take them to the park, play with them if they wanted. There was no tip-off that we were going to have trouble. But we did, and it started the very first day we moved in."

No Happy Endings

Rick was late in bringing his things to the new apartment, Carmen says. By the time he did arrive, it was noticeable that he had been drinking.

"He walked up to me and slapped me," Carmen says in a disbelieving tone. "I mean, the man just slapped me. I was so surprised, I couldn't even think. Then he started yelling at me, saying that there were some guys over at the Drake who wanted to see me, or something like that. I didn't know what he was even talking about. I had no business with any of those guys.

"Well, he was jealous, that's what he was. While I was standing there, holding my cheek that still was stinging, you know, he's telling me that so many guys were talking about me that he knows there must be something to it."

Carmen says that once he began talking and she finally realized that he had actually come into their home and struck her, she was devastated.

"It was more that my feelings were hurt," she says. "I mean, it hurt when he slapped me, but that wasn't the main thing. Here I'd been thinking all day that this was going to be a happy ending for the boys and me, that we had this guy who seemed to really care about us. I was so excited that I had a man who was so charming, so nice—and I'd met him so fast after getting here! I couldn't figure out what had changed, what had gone wrong."

Carmen serves dinner to her sons, Darrian and Parris. Carmen says she stayed with her boyfriend Rick because he was attentive and generous to her sons.

But why didn't she leave then? She was not married to him, nor had she had a long relationship with him. Quite the contrary; she had just met him! Why would she tolerate being physically assaulted?

Carmen thinks a while before answering.

"See, I guess I didn't want to be alone. I was in a new city, and even though I had made the trip without him, I realized how nice it was having someone right away. I didn't want to be by myself, worrying about everything. Like I said, afterwards I can look back and say that wasn't smart, or I should have done that different. But then . . . I could forgive a lot, as long as I had a man around who was good to me most of the time, and he sure was."

REGULATING HER FRIENDS

Once that night had passed, Carmen says that things went back to normal, at least for a while. Rick apologized for his violence, and he was attentive to her and the children.

"Then something amazing happened. I found out that in our building there was a girlfriend I'd known back in the projects in Chicago," she says. "It was so good to see a familiar face, and she was just downstairs from me.

"But he didn't want me going to see her, and he told me so. But I told him she was my friend and that nothing bad was going on. I wasn't seeing no guys down there or anything. But he got mad about it, and one night he took the rod out of the closet, you know, the rod you put hangers on? And he started hitting me with it, hitting me on the legs, making them all black-and-blue, with lumps on them. And he started yelling at me, how I was cheating on him. He even started spitting on me. It was like he was just so sure there was something he needed to be jealous of, even though there wasn't."

Carmen says that she accepted the beating for the same reasons that she accepted it the first time Rick slapped her.

"He was showing me his human side, I thought," Carmen says, frowning. "Sure, it hurt. But I figured his being jealous just proved how much I meant to him. I wish he'd shown it a different way. And now I know that what he was showing had nothing to do with love. But to me, although it hurt me, hurt my feelings, I didn't leave him.

"Maybe I would have if the boys had seen, but they hadn't. The kids were in the hallway playing, luckily. But after he finished hurting me, I called the police, and the boys saw Rick being taken away. Rick didn't try to fight it; he knew he was in the wrong. Like I said, the minute it was over, he was sorry. He'd say, 'I don't know what I was thinking of, Carmen.'

"But the kids sure knew what they were thinking of: they wanted to know why Rick was being led away by the police! They're saying, 'Where's Rick? Why are the police taking him?' I didn't really answer their questions. I was just worried that they were unhappy, and so I was trying to tell them that everything would be all right. Maybe if I'd tried to really explain to them, said out loud what he'd done, maybe I would have listened to myself and realize it sounded bad. But I didn't.

"He was in jail that time for two weeks, and he was released only after he promised that he would start attending these classes for people that couldn't control their tempers."

It was the same as before. Rick brought flowers and a beautiful pair of earrings. He begged her to forgive him and promised that he was a changed man.

"ALL NIGHT LONG"

"I accepted him back, and things were all right for a while," she says. "No beatings or batterings. We got along great. He was real affectionate, and to my mind, he loved me. Things were going fine until Rick and I went to this party in the building. It was just a get-together, nothing big. And even though I was with Rick the whole time, he started telling me in this soft voice that I was looking at these guys, and he wanted me to stop it.

"I wasn't looking at anybody," she protests, "but you couldn't tell him that. He wouldn't believe you. So when we came upstairs afterwards, we got into an argument almost right away. It scared me more than the other times, because he made me think he was going to throw me out the window. He took off the screen and opened up the outside window. I didn't know what was going to happen next.

"But he didn't do that. What he did was beat me up, not just slapping me, but punching me in the face. The beating went on all night. He told me at one point to take off my clothes. See, he was worried that if I was dressed, I'd go running out the door to get away. He took the phone out, too, so I couldn't call 911."

Carmen says that at one point Rick started dozing off, and she took advantage of the situation by running into the kitchen to get a knife.

"I couldn't find one fast enough," she remembers. "I only got a fork. I tried to stab him with it, but he came running in after me and took it away. He hit me again and told me to get back into bed before he hurt me worse than he already had. God, the beating went on all night long."

GETTING HELP FAST

When she looked at herself in the mirror the next morning, Carmen says, she was stunned at how different she appeared.

"My face was all swollen up, my lip was four times its size, and he'd punched me so hard in the side of my head that he broke my eardrum. I couldn't hear more than a tiny little bit; everything was muffled.

46

"I felt awful, and I just know that the boys had heard what was going on, especially Parris. I mean, they were asleep when Rick started in on me, but they couldn't have helped but hear. They were sleeping in the same room. I think Parris woke up during the night and heard the fight. He probably just pretended to be sleeping, though, so nothing would happen to him.

"It probably scared him to death," Carmen says slowly, thinking about that time. "And I wasn't paying attention to him, but I should have been. But I was so upset, so scared, that all I could

Carmen tends to the laundry while Parris and Darrian entertain themselves in the shelter's laundry room.

think about was trying to keep from getting hurt worse. That occupied me, you know, so I wasn't thinking like I should have been, thinking about my boys."

The next morning Rick left, leaving the phone. Carmen is sure that he intended to stay away, so he wasn't worrying about the police coming to take him away.

"I think he figured that he'd gone too far," she says. "He knew he'd crossed the line, you know? And I felt that way, too. I think it was looking at myself in the mirror that did it. I knew that things were getting worse, that if he really was sorry from the last time, why was it getting worse and worse?

Even though Rick would apologize after beating Carmen, she realized that the abuse was getting worse. That's when she decided to call for help.

"So the first thing I did was call First Call for Help [a crisis line]—it's right in the telephone book in the front. I can remember how mixed up I felt, dialing the number, worrying about what would happen to us. I packed a bag for me and the kids, and this battered women's shelter sent a cab to pick us up. I was rushing, running around real fast getting our stuff together. I didn't want to be still there when he came home, in case he wanted to start hitting me again."

"You Can't Stop Loving Him"

The staff at the shelter took pictures of Carmen's face and body when she arrived. These would be used as evidence, if and when she decided to press charges.

"Those pictures were so ugly," she says flatly. "I was so bad off, I couldn't even tell you where all those lumps and bumps in my head came from. There were so many. I couldn't move my head from side to side, it hurt so. My back hurt, my arms were bruised. I was ugly; I didn't even look like a human being.

"These advocates sat me down, helped me calm down. That helped a lot, because I felt so upset, you know? They asked me, did I want to get a restraining order for protection, so Rick couldn't see me or the boys? But I thought about it and I said no, I didn't. I think the people at that shelter were disappointed in me for that."

Carmen rolls her eyes toward the ceiling, as if searching for the words to make her point.

"See, in my mind, I still loved Rick. My kids cared about him. I know no one will believe this, or they'll say I must be stupid to think like that. But it's impossible to explain. If I were hearing this, I'd probably have trouble understanding it, too. But when you fall in love with someone, you just can't stop loving him. I mean, you may know some things in your brain, but your heart still holds on to him, you know?"

The Good 95 Percent

"It's kind of like with your kids. They can turn out to be bad, misbehaving every chance they get. And you can say that you don't like what they do. But you don't say you don't love them. It's like that with me and Rick. I don't know where the feeling of love comes from exactly. But I know that most of the time I was with him—95 percent of the time—I was happier than I'd ever been. He didn't hit me; he didn't yell or call me names. He was nice, paid lots of attention to me. It was like he was two different people, with two really different personalities. But the biggest part of him was the nice part, the part that was kinder and better than most women's husbands or boyfriends."

What exactly did he do that was so kind, so good? Carmen smiles.

"He'd cook for me, he'd clean for me. He'd take the kids places and do things with them when he could tell I needed a break. He didn't want me to have to do so much work around the house, even though that man was working two jobs. He'd say, 'Come on, Carmen, this is your day—relax.' That's what I loved about him, why I remember him as a nice man. He brought me flowers, always thinking of me. I'd never had anyone who was that nice to me before, not ever. That's why those advocates at the shelter couldn't understand me not getting a restraining order. All they saw was the bruises and the lumps, you know?"

"Used to Being Obeyed"

Carmen knew that as long as she stayed at the shelter she would be safe. It was a controlled environment, with set times the women and their children had to be in for the evening. Most importantly, each woman could be secure in the knowledge that the man who had abused her had no way of reaching her, unless a woman wanted him to.

"I had told my girlfriends where I was," she says. "I told them not to give my phone number out, no matter what Rick did. But I started hearing from them how Rick was so sad, that he really wasn't taking care of himself now that I'd gone. They told me he'd been losing weight, been letting his hair and beard grow. I heard this, and I told them, 'Give him my number.'

"The two of us talked on the phone, and he kept saying he wanted me to come home, that he was sorry and we should get back together. He was his own nice self, you know? But I told him no, that I didn't want to leave that shelter for a while. But see, even though that's what I meant *then*, I changed my mind kind of soon after that."

Carmen finally gave in to his wishes. She agreed to meet with him for a few hours. Nothing was resolved, however.

"At first it seemed like we were communicating, but that didn't last very long," she admits. "I was expecting him to say that he really understood what he'd been doing was wrong. But he didn't say that. He said he was sorry, but that's not the same thing.

"What he *did* say was crazy. I could tell that. He told me that it was *my* fault that he was getting violent and mean. He said that in his family, none of the women ever talked back to the men like I talked to him. He was used to being obeyed, like all of the guys in his family were. So I guess I could see where he got those ideas. Not that it made him right, though.

"So I told him that couldn't work with me, because I was my own person. I told him he wasn't my father or nothing, and that as long as I wasn't cheating on him or anything, I was going to make my own decisions about what I wanted to do or where I wanted to go. And I said that all of that didn't include him beating me up."

ANOTHER MEETING, ANOTHER BEATING

Carmen acknowledges that although that meeting left her with little hope that he was changing his attitude, she continued to meet him once in a while.

"It was only during the day," she says. "I'd meet him someplace and talk; and then I'd have to get back to the shelter by closing time. See, if I was late, I'd get kicked out of there. I usually took my kids with me, or else sometimes Parris was in school and I just took Darrian. And Rick came with me to the hospital, and was real nice, too, when I had to get my ear operated on, after that time he broke it.

"One time I said I would meet him in a more private place so we could talk. We agreed to meet at my girlfriend's house, but that was a real mistake. He started up the same old arguments again: how it was my fault because I argued with him. And I said the same old thing too: about how I was a person, and my opinions counted as much as his did. And then, well, he hit me, right in the eye."

She leans forward, pointing under her right eye.

"See," she says, her voice breaking, "I still got the bruise. This wasn't too long ago. And then he pushed me down the stairs, yelling at me the whole time. That time Parris and Darrian were right there, and they saw it all, plain as anything. He was saying that if I really loved him, then I'd stay and work this all out, instead of running away back to that shelter."

Carmen caresses Parris as he plays at the shelter. Carmen says she always stays to watch the boys play because any fights with the other kids may get her family kicked out of the shelter.

Asked whether it bothered her that her children had witnessed the violence, she nods.

"I didn't know what I know now, about how kids that come from homes where their mothers get beat up grow up to be batterers, too. Like I said before, I could listen to Rick talk about how all the women in *his* family obey their men, and now I know that, too. I know that's something he just learned, because that's the idea he grew up with.

"I hope it doesn't happen to my boys. I'd never want that. My main hope then, though, was to make sure they weren't upset, that they knew I loved them, and that Rick's temper didn't have anything to do with them being bad or anything.

"Anyway, I told Rick that I just wanted to get back to the shelter, and I had to get back to the bus station so I would be on time. It was a safe place for me, I told him, and we shouldn't be together like this. He kept it up, arguing, yelling. I was holding my eye and feeling kind of dizzy from the fall. And he started hitting me, punching me again. He even bit me here, on the hand. He hit me again in the eye, too, cut it open right here. I don't know why the punch ended up cutting me; he didn't have a ring or anything on."

PROFILE OF A BATTERER

When she got back to the shelter, the advocates there took one look at her and knew she had been with Rick again. They decided to pursue a more active role in teaching Carmen about batterers, since she still was unwilling to press charges.

"They counseled me again," she says, "but this time it made more sense to me. They told me that it made absolutely no sense for me to stay there in the evenings and go off and get beat up during the day, and I knew they were right. The people at the shelter explained some things about what they call the cycle of batterers, and that really fit Rick.

"They said that it was real common, and almost every couple that had this problem in their relationship went through the same things. The guy beats you up, first off. Then there's the honeymoon stage, where he is sweet, tells you how sorry he is, and how he'll never do it again. Then the tension builds up and he beats you again, and on it goes, around and around.

"They told me about some real common things batterers had in their personalities, and that seemed to fit Rick, too. And when this one woman told me how some batterers are really nice, generous, popular guys, and you'd never guess it about them, I sure agreed with that, you know?"

NOT THE FIRST TIME

As she listened to this information, Carmen began to realize that there was another part of Rick that fit the profile of a batterer: the idea that such violent patterns were often repeated, even when he started up a new relationship.

"He told me at first, you know, how he'd come up here to get a new life, and how he had 'girlfriend problems'? Well, as we got to know each other better, some things he said kind of struck me, you know? Like he said that he was wanted by the police back in Indiana, because he had been engaged to this girl, and he said he found her cheating on him. So he beat her up, took her car, and dropped her off on the highway. He did something with the car. I don't know what happened, but the car burned up.

"So he was wanted on counts of assault, kidnapping, and everything like that. But Rick thought that when they found out that the girl was his fiancée, not just some stranger, they might be easier on him. I don't know if they would, but that's what he thought. But it sure made me think, how he'd been doing this same stuff to some other woman before he did it to me.

"Anyway, I learned more than I ever knew before, but it really didn't make things easier. I still couldn't hate him for what he did to me. Me and the boys, we missed him."

Understanding

The meeting at her friend's house was one of the last times Carmen saw Rick. She has enormous difficulty in speaking about it. For almost a minute she can do nothing but look up at the ceiling, blinking back tears.

"I saw him maybe once or twice, but for a real short time," she says. "See, we lost the apartment. The lease was in my name, and since I was gone, he had to vacate. He ended up going to a chemical dependency shelter run by the Salvation Army. He did that on his own; nobody told him he had to. And he started taking these classes at the shelter.

"He was really *excited*, you know? He'd be calling me on the phone, telling me about how he was learning a lot of new stuff, same as I had at my shelter. He told me he understood now how that what he used to think was all wrong. He said he always thought it was never his fault, but now he was figuring out that wasn't true.

"They were showing him how he didn't have to hit me, that there were other things he could do when he got angry, things that wouldn't hurt anybody. I felt real hopeful after that, when we'd

Parris blows bubbles as his mother does laundry. Although Rick is out of their lives now, Carmen says that she and her sons continue to miss him.

get done talking on the phone. I was thinking that he sure is working hard and that things might get straight with us after all."

TOO LATE

Carmen never got the opportunity to see if Rick's new understanding of his anger would help their relationship. One evening, soon after they had talked on the phone, he was arrested while playing pool with some friends.

"The cops came in, looking for someone else," she says. "They asked all the guys there to show their IDs, and they ran them through their computer. They saw that he was wanted back in

Indiana, like I said before. He was extradited back there, to Gary, before I had a chance to see him or say good-bye.

"It's lonely here," she says softly. "He was the only person I had, except for that girlfriend. He was important to me. Even though he caused me heartache, he also made me happy. I think about him all the time, and I wonder if the two of us would have gotten back together. It seemed like we were so close. He really sounded like a changed man when we were talking on the phone.

"I've gotten two letters from him this week. He's only been in jail that long. He hasn't had his trial or anything, so there's no telling how long he'll be in jail. And who knows if he'll come back here after jail? Maybe he'll never see me again.

"I wrote him back, too. I told him that I believe people can change, that if they really want to get better, they can. If you want to change something bad about yourself, you can do that. It's too bad, though—bad luck, bad timing."

"It's Been Hard on the Boys"

She still has some of the bruises from their last fight, although those are fading daily. The bite marks are still visible. She says

Carmen leads Darrian into the elevator of the shelter. Life has been difficult for Carmen's sons, who witnessed their mother's beatings and suffering.

that she looks at them as reminders of the last time she and Rick were together and that it makes her sad.

"I can't do anything about Rick, I know that," she states. "It's him that has to change. And eventually, if he still comes around me, I'll have to make the decision whether it's a change for the better or not. I don't think I'd let myself go back into a relationship with him if it's going to be more of the same.

"But I can do something about Parris and Darrian. It's been hard on the boys, really hard. I mean, during the beatings, especially that last couple, both Parris and Darrian saw what happened. They were crying, saying stuff like 'Did Rick hurt you, Mama?' or 'Is he going to jail?' They didn't know what was happening to them, to me, or to Rick. And like I did before, I just was concentrating on them knowing things would be okay. I just kept saying that over and over.

"Parris is the one that changed the most, I know that. Darrian is littler, and he kind of bounces to the next thing. I know he remembers, but he can put that away, you know? But Parris is different. He was slow to talk when he was younger, and he's never had much to say. I always say I wish I'd read to him more; that would have helped him, his teachers said.

"And like I said before, Parris really liked Rick. Rick had that boy talking and giggling all the time. But since Rick's been gone— and even before that, since we left Rick for that shelter and had those big fights—Parris never has much to say. He acts different, too. He calls me Mommy now, and he never used to—just would tell me whatever he had to tell me. And he sits close to me, right up almost in my lap. Like he's some guard dog or something, making sure I'm okay. He's quieter than he ever was before, and I don't like to see that."

"SOMETIMES I GET SO STRESSED"

Carmen says that although she has no plans to get into another relationship with a man, she wonders what the boys' reaction will be if it were to happen.

"I think they'd be nervous about a new man, probably worried it would all start over again. Yes, nervous as can be. I think they'd be more protective than ever, probably scare anybody off who looked at me cross-eyed!

"I want to do right by my boys. I know I'm a better mother than I was to my older kids back in Chicago. I don't want to make the same kinds of mistakes, being too hard on them. But I'll tell you the truth, sometimes I get so stressed, and it will show on those kids. I yell at them. I do try not to spank them or hit them, because in the shelter, they told us it wasn't good.

"See, they want me to pay attention to what they're doing, usually at the times I can't think about that. They say, 'Watch me build this castle, Mama,' or 'Can you push me on the swing, Mama?' And then I tell them no, and I yell. That ain't good, I know that. What I should be doing is to talk to them real honestly, tell them that I'm not in a good mood now, but later I will do those things they want. But I'll tell you one thing: kids are smart. They can take advantage of a situation, like when you're real distracted or something. They can get away with stuff. They watch your eyes or something, I think!"

BIG PLANS

Carmen is not sure what the immediate future has in store for her. She wants to leave the homeless shelter as soon as possible for, as she says, they all need a real home.

"When we're settled, I want to get my high school diploma," she says with a smile. "That's actually one of my biggest plans. I'm going to get off welfare, too. I'm not sure what kind of a job I want, but I won't be real choosy. I want money so that I can put my own food on my own table and be proud of that. But I want to be smarter and have a diploma so I can have some choices, you know?

"Mostly, I want to have money to be able to do things that would be good for us. Like, I miss my grandfather and my other kids so much. So much! Yeah, I call them on the phone sometimes, long distance to Chicago, but it's almost worse talking to them. I'm so lonesome after I hang up I feel like crying. I haven't been telling my grandfather much of what's been happening up here, especially with Rick. He'd worry too much, and there's no point to that. There ain't nothing he can do four hundred miles away.

"So what I was thinking is maybe I'll save some money and buy me and the boys some bus tickets to Chicago, so we can go back for a visit. Maybe we'll catch one of those round-trip specials or something, like they advertise sometimes. That would be good for all of us, I think."

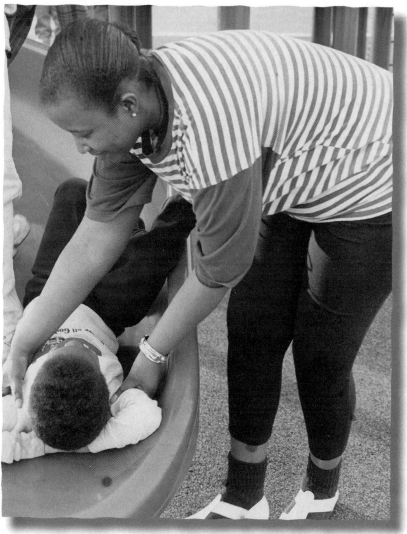

Playing with Parris is very important to Carmen. Now that Rick is gone, Carmen says Parris watches over her like a "guard dog."

"MAYBE NOBODY'D WANT ADVICE FROM ME"

If she could go back to that first day, when she and her sons got off the bus, how would she have changed things? Carmen wrinkles her brow, thinking very carefully.

"I know one thing, I'd start out by getting my own apartment with the boys. I wouldn't have made no deal with Rick about moving together. I'd have gotten to know him gradually. I'd date him, go about things lots slower. And I would try everything in my power to make things end up different.

59

"I'll tell you what. I'd give some advice to some young woman, maybe in the same position I used to be."

She interrupts herself and laughs.

"Maybe nobody'd want advice from me, right? I mean, I didn't do so good with my own life that I should be handing out advice to no other girls. But if I did, I'd tell them to get out of any relationship if a guy started beating them. It isn't right, and it sure isn't safe. I mean, there's lots of women that end up dead—way worse than me.

"But you also got to think about this: if the guy really is trying to change, going to classes and that, you can give him a chance. *A* chance, not lots of them. But be sure, and don't be in a hurry to take him back the same way as you got rid of him. The one thing I did wrong—the main thing—was to let him move in with me before we really knew each other. If I'd known earlier how he was, things would have turned out some other way.

The shelter has been instrumental in helping Carmen. With a nice place to stay temporarily and some food donations, Carmen has time to concentrate on herself, the boys, and the future.

"It's not your fault if he hits you; it ain't anything to do with you. It's all in him, the jealousy, the anger, all of that stuff. It isn't healthy for him to tell you it's your fault, 'cause you end up believing it a little bit, and then you're stuck. I guess it's only your fault if you keep staying with him if he don't ever change. You got to see something you believe in that will change, otherwise you're in the same mess every time. Don't you listen to him if he tells you he couldn't help hitting you, he just couldn't help it. I listened to that stuff for too long."

Carmen's eyes fill with tears again.

"But when you really love somebody it's hard to be right all the time. You got to know, when you are forgiving somebody, if that's smart or stupid to do. Each case is different, I know that. There were some times that I forgave too quick, I know that. But I still love him."

But is that really love, allowing herself and her children to remain in a dangerous situation? Carmen bristles, clearly defensive.

"No one can tell another person about love," she insists. "If I know down in my heart I love somebody, even if it's somebody you all hate, it don't matter. It's what *I* know that counts. And I have to be the judge of that, because who I decide to love, that's my business."

Lisa

"I DON'T WANT ANYBODY EVER TO
TAKE ADVANTAGE OF ME OR MY
KIDS. I KNOW OUR SOCIETY'S
VIOLENT. MY KIDS CAN LOSE A
FIGHT, BUT THEY SHOULDN'T
EVER JUST SIT THERE BEING A
VICTIM. THAT'S WHAT I DID, AND
THAT WAS THE BIGGEST MISTAKE
OF MY LIFE."

Lisa is distracted and uncomfortable, slumping self-consciously in
a kitchen chair. Her four children swarm around her, smiling
shyly at the visitors. The little boy, Pierre, steps on his younger
sister's toe, and she screams at him. Laughing, Pierre ducks into
the bedroom the four children share and locks it. His sister, still
screaming, pounds on it with her fists.

"Shut up, Shirley!" Lisa yells. "Pierre, come out of there. Now!"
She stands up abruptly and pounds on the door herself.

"Out, Pierre! I told you kids you had to be quiet!" she screams.
The door clicks open, and Lisa yells to her three daughters.

"All of you, inside here. Lay down in your beds, now!"

As her pouting children move slowly into the bedroom, Lisa
slumps back into her chair. She rubs her hands over her too pale
face and smiles apologetically.

"I told them kids I wanted it quiet so I could talk. They never
listen, but they're good kids. It's just that it's Saturday, and they
been in school all week, you know?"

"VIOLENCE IS A BIG PART OF MY FAMILY"

Lisa has recently removed herself from an abusive relationship with her boyfriend, Lawrence. When she finally left him, she went to a series of shelters, and when her allotted time ran out at the last one, she and her children tried staying at her brother's house for a while.

"That didn't work out; they didn't have no place for all of us," she says. "I really had nowhere to go after that, so I just went around to other shelters and ended up here, at this shelter. I have no idea whether Lawrence knows where I am. I hope he don't. I have no intention of seeing him ever again."

Lisa is relieved that she is done with him, but she says that in her life there have been relatively few times of peace, so she is not confident that the violent times are over for her.

"I'll tell you one thing: violence is a big part of my family. So much violence, so much abuse—it's all there. Some of it is just bad luck, like my cousin Sofia. She was outside the market and she got caught in cross fire and was shot. Man, she didn't deserve nothing like that. She was really good; her parents were really strict on discipline and curfews. She shouldn't have died. Bad luck, just being in the wrong place at the wrong time.

"And my little cousin—Hersey was his name—he got murdered by his parents. That was in all the papers. That all happened when I was eleven or twelve, I think. The parents, my aunt and uncle, were having a fight like they always did, and little Hersey ended up dead. Man, two years old! They claimed he fell down some stairs, but that was bull. I mean, he had been hit so hard that one of his balls had been pushed back inside him, and the coroner said that he took a hit in his stomach that was like a fall from an eighteen-story building.

"They got off, though, but everybody knew my uncle was the one that did it. He was so violent. But see, there's some law that husbands and wives don't have to testify against each other, and my aunt wouldn't. That was so terrible. I remember it so well."

"THAT'S THE TIME I STARTED REALLY HATING MY MOM"

Lisa grew up on the north side of the city, living with her mother and two brothers. She attended alternative schools, she says, because of some trouble she'd had as a girl. She refuses to elaborate.

"My mom had lots of boyfriends, and I remember we didn't like them much," she says. "The one named Dallas was the worst. He'd hit me and my brothers with sticks and paddles over really stupid things. I mean, like taking food out of the kitchen, or spilling something, or even running in the house. This all was when my mom had gone out, so she didn't see."

Did she try talking to her mother about that? Lisa shrugs.

"Yeah, we'd tell her, but she'd never do nothing then. So it just kept on. My younger brother Jimmy always got it the worst. He'd get beat every day by Dallas, whether there was a reason or not.

"That's the time I started really hating my mom," she says with a smile. "I mean, she was getting the same thing from that jerk.

Violence has been a part of Lisa's life since her childhood, when she was abused by one of her mother's boyfriends.

She'd be walking around with a bloody lip hanging there, not doing anything to leave him. Now that, I never asked my mom about, why she let him do that to her. All I knew is that by that night the two of them would be getting drunk again, and the hitting would start all over again. I hated her a lot."

Lisa seems lost in a trance, remembering. In a moment, she straightens up and smiles.

"The one good thing, though, is that she finally dumped him. I mean, really dumped him—on the highway. We had all gone to the zoo, my mom and Dallas and my brothers and me. Oh, and we had my little cousin Hersey then, too. In fact, that was the last time I saw Hersey. But anyway, Dallas was being really obnoxious the whole time. He'd been drinking, and he was really loud— yelling at us kids, using real bad language. I mean, this was in the middle of the day!

"So when it was time to go, she drove, and when we were out on the highway, she stopped and told him she'd had enough. She made him get out of the car. Dropped him right on the road. I guess it ended okay."

MEETING LAWRENCE

It was during her childhood on the north side that she met Lawrence. He and his family lived right across the alley, and although her friends warned her about him, Lisa found him interesting.

"He *was* a tough guy, really bad," she admits. "Plus he was four years older than me. My friends told me that he'd be trouble, because he ran with a gang and everything. It was the Disciples. But he didn't carry no gun or anything. He *did* carry a goat's leg, though. Yeah, a real goat's leg, with the hoof and the fur on it and everything. I guess it was to hit people with, or something. He just carried it around. It was a big old thing.

"I didn't like him right away. He kept asking me and asking me to go out with him, though. He'd ask in front of my friends, so I kind of got embarrassed and started going out with him. See, I wasn't a strong person then, not aggressive like I am today. No way. Lawrence made me what I am today, and I sure learned it the hard way.

"When I first got to know him, he didn't give any indication that he would be a batterer or anything. He was nice to me. During tenth grade he ended up living with us. That was about two months after we started going together. Yeah, he stayed right in my room, slept with me."

Did her mother know what sort of arrangement was going on? Lisa shrugs again.

"Yeah, she knew, but she didn't care. She was wild herself, though. She drank, ran around with her boyfriends. I mean, it wasn't like she set no shining examples, you know? She couldn't tell me what to do if she wasn't doing it. Anyway, my one brother liked him a lot. In fact, he still does. My other brother couldn't stand him. We got along okay. I guess we got along better than okay, because I got pregnant that same year, when I was fifteen!"

JAIL AND A CHANGED PERSONALITY

When Lisa was still pregnant with her first child, Lawrence and his friends were out drinking one evening and were stopped by the police.

"They were looking for him," she says, "because he'd been accused of having sex with a minor. Not me, another fifteen-year-old girl. And it didn't help that he had like a thousand dollars' worth of stolen stuff in the car with him. Stereo stuff, clothes, even tires—so they put him in jail. He ended up staying for two and a half years, then another two years on parole.

"But hey, I was mad at him, so what did I care? I was pregnant and thinking he loved me, while he was out doing stupid things like having sex with other girls. So really, I didn't even care what was going to happen to him. I just figured I would raise that kid on my own, that's what I'd do."

However, after he was released from jail, Lawrence returned to Lisa, hoping they could get their relationship back on track. Although she says she could kick herself now for being so weak, Lisa forgave him.

"By that time, baby Shana was born, so I was a lot more forgiving than I was at first," she admits. "I wanted to get things going, too. Having a baby around seemed like a reason to have him, too. I mean, he was her father, and that seemed important at the time. And, plus, he promised me that there'd be no more having sex with other girls.

"At first, it seemed like things would work out, but then he started using crack. Crack is what ruined Lawrence. Or at least made him worse.

Lisa gets a kiss from her daughter Shana during a routine smoke break. Occupants of the shelter can't smoke or drink in their rooms.

He changed so much from the way he'd been before. I mean, he wasn't perfect, I know that. But to me he'd always been pretty nice. No hitting, no yelling. But man, that changed.

"It got real obvious that he didn't care about nothing but his crack. He'd lie, steal, take anything he could get money for, so's he could buy that stuff. He took my food stamps and cashed them in with some guy he knew would give him money for them. That would go for drugs.

"He got into this real racist thing, too. He hadn't been that way before; at least I'd never heard him. But he started calling white people all devils, saying they were all bad and out to get him. Part of that was the crack talking, but I know part of that was him, too. I started really getting scared of him. Like I said, I was lots sweeter then, I'd never say *anything,* even when I should have."

WHEN THE BATTERING STARTED

Lisa says that although he hadn't hit her yet, she could sense that violence was becoming a threat. The hitting started, she says, when Lawrence began cheating on her again.

"One time Lawrence's mom and me, we were sitting in the living room. Lawrence and his friend Demitrius came in, and Lawrence asked me if he could have five dollars. I mean, he never had no job, so he was always out of money. But I told him yeah, and I gave him the money. Anyway, a minute later I look out the window, and there's the car outside, and there are two girls in it!

"So later on, he came in and he knew that I knew what was going on. So he deals with it by taking the offensive, you know what I mean? *He* starts yelling at *me*! And he didn't stop at yelling, neither. He told me to get my ass out of bed, and he keeps yelling and then starts hitting me on my bare leg as I'm getting out of bed. He was real grumpy, real mean. That was the first time, like I said.

"And it kept going from there. It got worse as it kept up. I mean, like one day he was out in the back working on the car. He had come in for a second to get something and then was going back outside. He said some mean thing to me, something real smart. Well, I yelled back at him. So he turned and ran back up the stairs towards me and grabbed my neck. He kept banging my head against the wall, and it hit on the edge of that door molding.

"Then he dragged me into the bedroom and threw me on the bed. He kept doing the same thing, banging my head into the backboard of that bed. He called me bad names—bitch, whore, blue-eyed devil—whatever came into his mind. Boy, that hurt a lot! I had lots of knots there in the back of my head where it didn't show, but don't think I couldn't feel it all the same. I had the majorest headache I ever had in my life. Lawrence was convinced I was cheating on him, and he said that that was why he was hitting me. It wasn't true, though. I never cheated on him. But now, man, I wish I had!"

WORSE AND WORSE

Lisa says that as time went by, she knew that they had fallen into a very predictable pattern. Lawrence would be nice to her, then the stress and tension would begin to show in him until it erupted into a beating. Immediately afterwards, she says, he was sorry and begged for forgiveness.

"Yeah, 'sorry' was his favorite line," she says with a bitter laugh. "And he was good at it—acted like he really meant it. I'd forgive him, thinking things would get better, since he seemed to know he'd done something real wrong. Inside, I guess I wanted things to get better so much that I'd sort of fool myself into believing they actually were, you know? So I tried to make things pleasant, and then my kids would have a good home. But the real thing was fear. I didn't want to get killed, and Lawrence always threatened to come after me if I tried to run. So I didn't.

"But then, other stuff would happen, like him cheating on me again, this time with my best friend. Oh, he denied it, but I'm not stupid. We had been celebrating his birthday the night before at my mom's house. We were living upstairs then, and when I started feeling sick, I just lay down there and went to sleep. The next morning I went upstairs to my room, and there were my girlfriend's clothes all over the floor by the bed. He denied it, like I said, but I know. I mean, even if she had slept over, why in *our* bed, and why did she have her underwear off and tossed all over like that? So he did that."

Remembering the long string of abuse and cheating is hard for Lisa. She recalls that after each beating her boyfriend Lawrence would apologize and beg for her forgiveness. "'Sorry' was his favorite line," Lisa says.

The financial situation was getting worse, too. The lack of money, due to Lawrence's selling of Lisa's food stamps, added stress between them. So was the fact that Lawrence refused to get a job.

"Oh, he'd never work," she says with a dismissive wave of her hand. "The only time he'd get some job was when he needed to show on paper that he was employed—part of his parole agreement, I think. So he'd work for a few days out at the airport. I mean, he was so bad, he couldn't even make money selling drugs. He kept smoking up what he was supposed to be selling, and then we'd be worse off."

When Lawrence and his brother were arrested—she isn't certain for what—Lisa says that it was a welcome relief.

"I was just glad he was gone. It was like a breather. By that time I think we had two more kids, so it was nice for him to be gone— all his yelling and hitting and everything. At that time we were living with his brother's girlfriend, and that was hard. See, we were always looking for somewhere else to stay, because we had no money. If he'd have left my food stamps alone, we might have been able to afford a place. It wears on you, though, after a while. But Lawrence was not going to change, and the government sure as hell wasn't going to start giving me more money!"

"He Would Get Really Evil"

If she had any hopes that jail would have a positive effect on Lawrence, Lisa soon found out differently. He began drinking more, using more crack, and as a result, becoming more abusive.

"It was like a split personality thing," she explains, "like that Dr. Jekyll and Mr. Hyde or whatever. He'd be okay one minute, then he'd go out with his brother and be drinking that hard liquor, and he'd come home mean. I mean, he would get really evil, really cruel.

"One night he was at a party and came home late. I was sitting up watching television. I tried not to meet his eyes because I didn't want him coming after me. See, lots of times part of the battering would be forcing me to have sex, too. I hated it; it was horrible. So I was just trying to avoid his eyes, but he got mad anyway. He threw a pan of hot mushroom soup at me. The kids were still babies, and so they didn't know what was going on, thank goodness.

"I knew he would really hurt me. I could just sense that. He was poking me real hard with his fingers and yelling. He poked me right in my eye, too. See? He broke a blood vessel there, and it's still there."

Lisa points to a bruised area under her right eye. She smiles.

"But I got him! I head butted him that time, right into his hand that was doing the pointing, and I messed up his fingers. I was glad I did that, and I think it sort of surprised him. It's not like he stopped hitting me, but he did stop that time."

"He Really Did a Number on Me"

Did she never think to leave Lawrence? Didn't she worry that one of his beatings could kill her? Lisa nods, as though she has been expecting that question.

"See, it's real hard to explain to someone who's never been through that. I'm not just some stupid person who wants to be hit or yelled at and threatened. But I was kind of trapped—at least I felt that way a lot. I didn't have money and I didn't have a job, since I was raising these four kids. I mean, to them, he was their daddy."

But why wouldn't she leave? Surely she could do better than having a boyfriend like Lawrence? She takes a deep breath.

"The biggest thing is that he really did a number on me," she says. "When I told him I couldn't take no more of that and that I was going to leave him, he'd just shake his head and laugh at me. He'd tell me over and over how ugly I was and how no man would ever want me, because I had the four kids. Nobody would want me, nobody would want me, I was ugly."

Lisa's eyes fill with tears but she swipes them away angrily with the back of her hand.

"Man, when they do that, boy . . . that works after a while. I believed it. My—what do you call it—self-esteem? That was shot to hell. Over and over again: you're not wanted, you're no good. And then you get to the point of not knowing anything anymore. I mean, I *thought* I was a good person. Weak, maybe, but good. But after Lawrence telling me over and over how bad and ugly I was, I really didn't know anymore."

Lisa says that although he claimed she was completely undesirable, he certainly acted like a jealous boyfriend.

"It was so funny, because any time he thought I was gone too long, he'd get mad, jealous. One time we were walking home from the store, and some guy looked at me. Lawrence was so mad. He

Lisa's children were also affected by Lawrence's violence. He would abuse the kids and leave them alone when he was supposed to be watching them.

thought the guy must be looking at my hair, and that pissed him off. See, I used to have really long, curly hair, down to my waist.

"Anyway, when we got home, that sucker cut my hair right off. Can you believe that? Just got a scissors and chopped it off. It looked really uneven, really horrible, like some little kid did it. I was so frustrated then. If I got mad, it would make him worse the next time, and he might go after one of the kids. That was what I feared. I remember crying, cleaning up that hair all over the floor, worrying about what I could do."

HE WAS A TERRIBLE FATHER

As she feared, Lawrence eventually began turning his anger on the children. At first, she says, it was apparent in his unwilling-ness to watch them when Lisa was busy. Eventually he began beating them, too.

"I was so mad this one time," she recalls. "I had started going back to night school, working on my GED. I wanted to be able to get a job and support my kids. But I'll tell you, even though people say that it's easier to go back to school when you're older, that wasn't true for me. It was worse than when I was a kid living at home with my mother and brothers and Lawrence. I couldn't concentrate at all, having the kids and Lawrence, worrying about everything.

"I started not being able to go to school. Every time I'd leave, he'd take off, leave the kids alone. I mean, at this point I had a baby that was just three weeks old, and the others were still little, too! I didn't know he was doing that at first. But one time I arranged for my cousins to come over to feed the baby, since Lawrence didn't want to do that part.

"Anyway, they came over just when they were supposed to, but he wasn't there at all. The kids didn't know where he was, and they were scared. Well, he came back after a while, and my cousins were there waiting for him. They started yelling at him, telling him how that wasn't right, that he was endangering his kids by leaving them tiny ones like that. They told me about it afterwards, my cousins did.

"But he ended up doing worse. I mean, my kids weren't bad, not like they seem now."

Family dinners are very important to Lisa. She makes the kids turn off the television during dinnertime and makes sure that they clean their plates.

She pauses to bang on the closed bedroom door. "Keep quiet in there!"

"Anyway, they were just little, having fun in a small apartment, you know? They'd run around, play. Sometimes someone would fall and cry, but that was easy to solve. But he'd beat them for doing that stuff, just like Dallas did to us kids when we were younger. He'd take a toilet brush, you know, with the bristles? He'd hit them over and over on their legs until they were bruised and had bloody scratches all over them.

While the older kids are at school, Lisa and her daughter Shirley run errands. Shirley tries to keep herself amused during the long wait at the government offices.

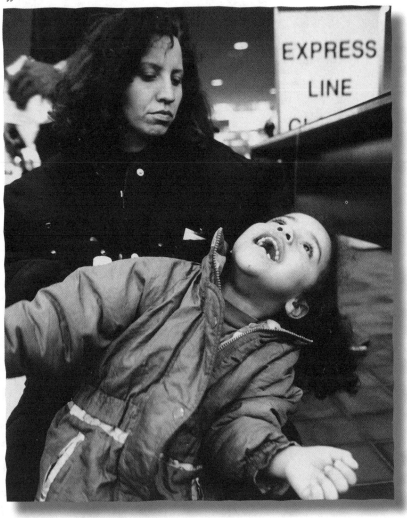

"I wasn't around for some of it, but some of it I was. I was scared of him, and I'm not saying it was right. I was afraid. I knew my kids were hurting, but I needed to choose the right time to leave so he couldn't follow us. Yeah, it made me sad that they were getting hit. It made me sad that *I* was getting hit, too. But I just kept telling myself that we were going to get away somehow, as soon as we could. We'd run and never come back."

Taking the Children Away

The opportunity came very soon, but not until after Lisa and her children went through a very painful incident, one that began with Lawrence.

"I had taken our dog, Butch, to the store in the morning, before Shana was supposed to leave for school. She went into the bathroom and was messing with my razor, and she cut some of her hair off. Lawrence got real mad at her, took his belt off and beat her on the upper thighs with the buckle.

"I had been gone, like I said, so I didn't know what happened. After it all happened, I thought about how sad she must have been, going off to the bus, probably crying, or trying not to, knowing Shana. She's an independent little thing, takes pride in doing everything for herself.

"Anyways, she went to school, and while she was there she had an accident—wet herself. See, she had a bladder infection at the time, and sometimes that happened. Well, when the school nurse was helping her out of her wet clothes, she noticed Shana's bruise, really bloody and ugly looking. That lady told the school officials, and they called the cops."

The first she knew anything was amiss was when she was waiting for the school bus that afternoon.

"I was getting worried, because it was later than usual," she says. "I was standing there, looking out the window, and my mom was over there, too. It got later and later, and then it came. But right behind it was a police car, with Shana in the back!

"The cops got out and came to the door, told me they were taking the rest of my kids away. Now, Lawrence hadn't told me nothing about beating her, only that he had yelled at her about the razor. So I didn't have any idea what the cops were doing. All hell broke loose.

"Shana was scared, the dog was running around, I was flipping out. Butch really likes my son Pierre, and when one of the cops tried to pick him up, Butch bit the cop. They got mad, told me that I'd better watch out, or they'd shoot the dog. So my brother, who had come by, solved it by picking Pierre up and carrying him out to the police car."

Not Protecting Her Children

Lisa says that the whole thing made her upset—from Lawrence's cruelty to Shana to the insensitivity of the police.

"I can't explain how horrible it was, seeing my kids be taken away from me. They were crying, reaching out for me. But no, even though it was Lawrence who did it, I was the one being punished. He acted like he could care less. And I was the one who was accused of being unfit, because I couldn't protect the kids!

"When I found out what Lawrence had done to Shana, I was furious. And Shana didn't lie; she told the police that her father had done that to her. So off the kids went, for protection from their stupid father and me. It was hell, going through the next few days."

After three days, Lisa says, her children were released, except for Shana. She had tearfully told the social workers that she was afraid to go home because of what her father might do.

"They came home from the shelter, but not to their home. The authorities didn't believe they'd be safe with me, and so they were put in my mom's custody for a while. My mom let me have them sometimes, because she knew how much they meant to me. But when Lawrence came home the day they were released, he got mad.

"He walked in, carrying some laundry he'd been doing. He doesn't say a word, just looks at them. When he notices that Shana isn't there, he comes over to me and punches me right in the face. He said, 'Where's my daughter? She has no right to be gone! Those people have no right to take her from me'—stuff like that. Like I told you, it's not like he was worrying about her at all while the kids were gone.

"Anyway, that night I got a beating like I never had in my life. He yelled, called me the same old names, told me how white people were evil, and that I wasn't allowed to have any white girlfriends from now on. He punched me, kicked me, dragged me around by my hair all through the house. I was screaming and crying, and the worst of it was that my kids were standing there the whole time, watching from their bedroom door. I ran into the bathroom after he was through, and tried to clean myself off, take a bath. Man, those bruises hurt, especially with that hot water!

"Afterwards I looked at myself in the mirror, and I just felt sick to my stomach. I mean, he was right. I *did* look ugly, with those bruises, my puffy eyes, my bloody mouth. God, I looked bad."

TO THE SHELTER

Lisa took Shana, who was staying with Lisa's mother, to the doctor the next day. Her daughter had an appointment because of the bladder infection. After taking one look at Lisa, however, the doctor was just as concerned about her.

"At the clinic they saw me, knew I'd been beaten," she says. "I'd tried to hide it—putting my hair down so it hid my face—but it didn't work. They asked me if I wanted to press charges, and I said yes. I wanted Lawrence to go to jail, because I knew it was just going to keep going the way it was, and nothing was going to improve. Plus, I'd been giving some of my check money to my mom to hold for me, and Lawrence was mad because he wasn't getting his drugs.

"So they took pictures of my face, and the police came over there, right to the clinic, and took my statement. They drove me back to my house so I could get some clothes and things before the kids and me could go to the shelter. Lawrence was there, just sitting around in his bathrobe. He was acting like nothing was wrong at first, but when I started packing, he came after me. I mean, the police were right there, and he's going to hit me! They grabbed him, and he kept fighting them. My kids were all yelling, 'My daddy, my daddy,' because they thought he would get beat up by the cops.

"But we left, and Lawrence went to jail for a while. I didn't care for the shelter much, though. I stayed three weeks, but I was ready to leave. It was nice being safe and everything, but I know they didn't like me there. I mean, they wanted me to tell all about myself, what Lawrence did, how I felt, what was going on. But I didn't want to tell them all my business, you know? It just wasn't their right to hear all that, so I didn't. I probably should have talked to them, but I wasn't ready. I talked to a psychologist, and that was okay. But the people at the shelter, they were all set to judge me."

Lisa sighs, rubs her forehead.

"You know, they have good intentions, but they don't get it. I got mad at them. I mean, they don't know what it's like. They go on what they hear, everything like that. But they don't know what it's like to be afraid, to be worried that he was going to whup the kids if I did something. I just didn't trust them, I guess. I was trying the best I could. I knew that, even if they couldn't see it."

Didn't she realize that getting herself and her children away from Lawrence was her responsibility? Lisa smiles tightly.

"Sure I did," she says. "It was me that had to do something. I just didn't know what would work, though. He wouldn't let a little thing like a restraining order or some piece of paper stop him, though. No judge was going to save me, not unless they slapped him in jail forever. No, it was my job, and I worried about it every night, not sleeping, not eating much. Just worrying."

"MY STEPPING-STONE"

After leaving the shelter, Lisa met a man named Jerry, whom she still speaks of with affection.

"He was a good, good friend," she says with a smile. "He wasn't violent, wasn't mean. He was good for me. He's got a girlfriend now, but I wish him all the luck in the world. He was my stepping-stone, Jerry was. He tried to undo all that garbage talk that Lawrence had done on me. Jerry told me I was pretty. He told me I wasn't a whore at all and that I was really worth something. I mean, he kept telling me that all the time. I really needed to hear those things from someone, and he was there for me.

"I saw Lawrence when I got out of that shelter, although it sure wasn't me looking for him. My stupid brother found out and told him. My brother is such a loser, just like Lawrence. The two of them hang out together, sucking weed and drinking from the time they get up till they go to bed. Next time I move, I'll never, never tell my brother."

Lisa shrugs when asked about the restraining order. Wasn't he breaking the law by coming to see her or the children?

"He didn't care," she snorts. "He did what he wanted. He was trying to get an end to that order anyway, so he could at least see his son. But I didn't want him anywhere near us.

"He even went so far as to take the kids, during the day, right out of school. The school screwed up big time, too, because it says clear as anything on that emergency card you fill out, you know?

78

Lisa cooks fried chicken for dinner in the shelter's kitchen. She says she is constantly running from Lawrence. "If he knows where I am, me and the kids are doomed."

He's not listed as caregiver; he has no custody to take those kids. But the school released them, and he took them to his neighborhood and enrolled them in school near him.

"He had them not even a month, and he wasn't enjoying having them around. I found out that he'd been whupping them again. He'd whup them for peeing or for crying for me—lots of stuff. But I wanted them back, and I fought him on it, and I won. The schools knew that they'd made a mistake, and Lawrence was going to get in a lot of trouble if it got reported, so he let me take them back."

THE LAST TIME

Lisa says that although she made no moves to reconcile with Lawrence, he continued to come to the house. The final time, she states, was one evening when he came over, presumably to see the children.

"He raped me," she says simply. "The kids were in the house, but I don't think they saw. He ripped my clothes off me and had his hands around my throat. He was saying all kinds of threats, telling me that no matter what I did, I'd always belong to him. Plus, he told me that everything was my fault. That was a big deal for him. It was my fault he went to jail, it was my fault he was always yelling at me, it was my fault he had to get rough.

"That's garbage, though, and I know it. But I sure as hell wasn't going to hang around there and have him coming over all the time. He'd kill me, I do believe that. Maybe not if someone was around, but if I was alone, yeah, he'd do it.

"So I went to another shelter and then to my brother's—not the one who's friends with Lawrence, the other one. But he didn't have room for us there, not for me and the kids. So now I'm here, waiting to find a place. I hope to God he doesn't know where I am. I'm really serious about that. I'm not worried that I'm going to cave and forgive him. No way. That's done. But he'll keep coming after me, and if he knows where I am, me and the kids are doomed."

Lisa says that she intends to move to another part of the city and eventually leave town altogether.

"I'm going to change the kids' names," she says. "But don't put down what they've chosen; I don't want him reading about it. Not that I think he could read it or anything. I don't want him to get even a hint. I know there's no way he'd give up tracking us down."

A MORE VIOLENT PERSON

Lisa's children are getting antsy again, and they are inventing reasons to tiptoe out of their bedroom.

"Mama, he hit me," accuses Shirley in a quavering voice.

"Get in there," yells Lisa. "I'm going to give you a spanking if you don't!"

"Mama, there's *blood*," Shirley wails softly.

Her mother is having none of it, however. Jumping to her feet, she propels her youngest daughter into the bedroom and slams the door. When she returns, she is philosophical.

"You know, I can tell that all of this stuff has made me a more violent person. I never really was before. But now, lately, if someone's mistreating me, or if some boyfriend is acting all smart with me, I lash out. My kids, too, they get their spankings. But I'm mainly talking about guys.

"I mean, right now I have a boyfriend. We argue a lot. And when I get mad, I hit him. I know I've got to stop that, because I'm just asking for trouble, asking to be hit back. It's a mistake, because I'm hoping this guy will be the one. I'm hoping he'll be my husband eventually, be a good father to the kids. It's hard doing everything on my own and to try to do a good job, you know?"

"Lawrence Is Like a Ghost in My Head"

What would she do if her current boyfriend started behaving as Lawrence had? She shakes her head.

"I'd hit him, that's what I'd do. In fact, this already came up, not long ago. I went out with my girlfriend to celebrate her birthday, and afterwards he started saying some stupid stuff. I started punching him in his face. And he hit me back, and I don't blame him. Like I said, I got to cut that out. But Lawrence is like a ghost in my head, turning my head all the time. I think to myself, I'm not going to take anything like that from nobody else, not ever again. No one's ever going to hit me or my kids again.

"You know, last week the principal at Shana's school and me, we got into it on the phone. Shana got into a fight at recess trying to defend herself. I teach my kids that: don't ever stand there and let somebody hit you or whatever. Give it back, I say.

"But this principal was telling me about no fighting, no hitting, or whatever. I told that principal I don't agree with that, that I want my daughter to be defending herself, especially against some boy. He'd been kicking her, pulling her hair. She even got a knot right on her head. But she did like I told her and punched him in the mouth—made his lip bleed.

"So both of them got suspended, but I'll tell you, I'm proud of her. She's a strong-willed little thing. But that principal yelled at me, told me I was condoning violence."

Does she? Does she think that teaching her daughter to fight back on the playground is the right thing to do?

Lisa pauses a moment, thinking.

Lisa says she is tired of being a victim. From now on, she is going to fight back and teach her kids to do the same.

"I don't want anybody ever to take advantage of me or of my kids. I know our society's violent. And some people might say that fighting back is just adding to it. But getting beat up, and taking it—jeez, that just teaches the one who's hitting that he can get whatever he wants just by being tough. My kids can lose a fight, but they shouldn't ever just sit there being a victim. That's what I did, and that was the biggest mistake of my life."

Mary

"I'M SMARTER THAN I USED TO BE. I KNOW I DON'T NEED TO BE WITH NO MAN THAT BEATS ME OR IS MEAN TO MY KIDS. I'M NOT AFRAID OF HIM NO MORE, AND I KIND OF LIKE THE IDEA OF US BEING ON OUR OWN IN A NEW CITY."

She is outside, sitting on a bench, having a late-morning cigarette. A Reader's Digest volume, entitled *The Most Mysterious Places on Earth*, is occupying her, and she doesn't notice her guest approach. Surprised at the sound of her name, Mary looks up and smiles. In the way of many poor people, she carefully rubs the hot tip of her cigarette along the bench and puts it in her purse. She will save the last half for another time.

"Man, I been engrossed in that book," she says, standing up and shaking hands. "I have always loved to read, and that one is a good one. I like reading about those places—Stonehenge, places like that. Plus, it feels so good to be outside, now that the kids are back in school!"

"WE WERE HAVING PROBLEMS BACK IN CHICAGO"

Mary and her four youngest children have come from Chicago's south side. She left behind a husband who beat her and her children and, she suspects, had been molesting one of her daughters. She has made the move hoping to find a place where, she says, "the schools are better, and people are nicer."

"We were having problems back in Chicago," she explains. "I been with that man for eight years, and I left him. I'm smarter than I used to be. I know I don't need to be with no man that beats me or is mean to my kids. I'm not afraid of him no more, and I kind of like the idea of us being on our own in a new city."

However, as Mary admits, things have not started out well in her new life. Upon arriving from Chicago, she found an apartment on the north side of the city that used up much of her savings.

"It was a dump," she says matter-of-factly. "I was paying five hundred dollars a month for the place, and it didn't even have a stove or refrigerator. I was working part-time, but that's all. See, I've got small kids, and I didn't want to be gone when they were home from school.

"I managed for a while, for a couple of months, anyway. I made friends with a lady downstairs; her name was Jackson. She let me put some food in her refrigerator. And I got an electric skillet to

Mary reads constantly. "I just can't get enough books. Everyone keeps stealing the ones I have," she says with a laugh.

cook some things. But it didn't work out. Kids need more than fried food, and that lady downstairs was eating my food.

"That man who owns those buildings gets away with it, being a slumlord. I hear they have tried to close him down lots of times, but he gets out of it every time. And this isn't the only raggedy old building he owns. He's got lots of them.

"That was no way to live, anyway. And I know the way we were living back in Chicago was no way, either. I guess if I had to choose, though, I'd take this. At least I've got no mean man jumping on me, hitting me and the kids. *That's* the worst."

"I DIDN'T GROW UP WITH NO VIOLENCE"

Mary's upbringing was far different from that of her children, she says. She was raised by a loving grandmother, and she was very happy.

"My mother, all her people, were from down south, so I've been told," she says. "I never knew my father. And my mother didn't raise me; she came up to Chicago with me and my three brothers. She gave me to my grandmother to raise, while she took the boys and lived somewhere else in the city.

"Did I feel abandoned? Not at all, not at all. I mean, my mother came to see me. It wasn't like I never saw her. But my grandmother loved me—I was her little girl! I was so happy then. I didn't grow up with no violence, no man pushing people around. My grandmother was real strict. We went to church all the time. She always dressed me up real nice. But she had her rules! I couldn't go no further than the corner when I was playing, and I had to be home before the lights outside came on.

"She died when I was ten, of cancer. She'd been in the hospital; she was real, real sick. And after that I went to live with my mother and my three brothers. You know, I was thinking about this just the other day. That was the time my life really changed, when I got around her and especially my brothers."

Mary laughs, shaking her head.

"Boy, my brothers really turned me out, in a way. I started staying out late because we didn't have no strict rules at my mother's. Within a year I had me a boyfriend. I was getting into all kinds of trouble I ain't even seen at my grandmother's. I think about it now. I wish that she hadn't died then, so I could have stayed with her longer. I'd have been a different person; I know I would."

A Teenager with Three Kids

Despite the differences between her mother and grandmother, Mary says that she loved her mother.

"She was an alcoholic, my mother was," she says. "In fact, I think most everybody in my family was. But she was cool, she was fine. She had her boyfriend, and they ran a little candy store over on the south side, right on the corner. And I'll tell you, we didn't want for nothing when I was little. We always had what we needed; we was never hungry, always had good clothes. That's why today money doesn't excite me too much, not like the people who grew up without food, without things. That wasn't me."

Lack of supervision, however, resulted in her becoming pregnant at the age of fourteen, again at sixteen, and once more at seventeen.

"It wasn't surprising, I guess," she says with a wry smile. "I mean, we had friends over all the time when my mother was working at that store. I had my boyfriends, my brothers had girlfriends—you know how it goes.

"I left home at eighteen, because I could have my own welfare check. I had three kids—Demetria, Augustus (Gus), and Christopher—and we moved into our first apartment on our own. I'd been trying to still go to school, at least on and off, but I finally stopped trying. It was just too hard, with the kids and all. I stayed in that apartment a while and moved again. By this time I was pregnant with my fourth; that would be my daughter Latrice. Just as I was moving into this new place, that's when I met Lee."

A Man's Man

Mary admits that she found Lee very attractive at first. In addition to being handsome, he was quite a bit older than she.

"I met him through my brother. He introduced me to Lee, brought him right up on the porch where I was sitting, just taking a break moving in to the apartment. I hadn't shopped for food yet, but Lee got right up and went over to the food store and bought some groceries for me. I'll tell you, I was impressed.

"He was thirteen years older than me, had himself a car and a good job. He was a carpenter, getting jobs doing the finishing on buildings around the city. And he sometimes did furniture, too, so he was always busy. He was tall and in shape, real good-looking.

"But hey," she says with a laugh, "I was real cute, too. In my shorts you know, I looked fine. I had three kids already, but I

Mary rarely joins her children for dinner. Instead, she sits on the couch and chats with them about their days in school.

didn't look it. And it didn't seem to bother him that I had these kids and another on the way. That impressed me, too."

When she and Lee finally moved in together, she found him to be less than easy to live with, however.

"I don't mean he was abusing me or anything," she says quickly. "He wasn't bad or nothing, just not as friendly and easygoing as he'd seemed. He wasn't what you'd call sweet to me, or anything. He was kind of grumpy, you know, had kind of a mean streak. I thought his being kind of mean was all right. He wasn't a push-over, like some men are. He was a man, and I liked him for that."

LEARNING TO STAY HOME

Lee began the abuse about seven months after they began living together.

"He'd shown me a few signs," she says. "I knew before the actual hitting and battering started he was capable of that. I mean, he had himself a temper, even though he hadn't taken it out on me or the kids. But the main thing I was noticing more and more was this jealous side of him. He started asking me where I was going, where I been, stuff like that.

"He even had his friends spy on me when he was at work or over visiting his mother, or something. I'd go down in the basement to see some friends of mine or go to the store. When he'd get home, he'd be, like, 'Why'd you go to the store?' 'Who you talking to downstairs?' I'd be so confused at first—I wondered how he knew where I'd been. But I knew I hadn't been doing anything wrong, so I wasn't worried about that. His friends, his spies, must have told him that. It made me mad, though, him knowing every move I made.

"I don't remember when his being jealous and mad turned into him hitting me. I know it was when we still lived in that building, that first one. It wasn't about anything real. It was just the same old thing—where I'd gone or something like that. See, he expected me to be home in the house all day, doing nothing, I guess. I mean, it was me and the kids, just sitting there. We weren't supposed to go out, not to the park, not to the store, not to visit friends. Sometimes we did go out, and it would lead to fights."

Did she think about leaving then? Mary shrugs self-consciously.

"I'll tell you, I kind of figured it was a rare thing, you know? I mean, everything else was okay. I guess I was willing to forgive some of that."

"HE SORT OF BROKE MY SPIRIT"

Mary says that Lee would slap her and call her ugly names and that eventually she did as he asked.

"After a while, I stayed in most of the time, just like he wanted," she says. "I just got tired of the fighting, got tired of it all the time. I just couldn't go through it every day, knowing I would get hit. He'd slap me in front of his friends, try to show off like a big man. It was just easier to give in. He sort of broke my spirit, I guess you could say."

Why did she stay then? Mary smiles broadly.

"I loved him!" she says with emphasis. "He was a man; he was older than me. He was a good provider, even though he was mean sometimes. I mean, me and my kids didn't want for nothing, as long as we stayed in the house. And other than being jealous sometimes, he was good to me. It wasn't always bad, not every day or anything like that.

"And see, I don't want you thinking I *liked* getting beat up, because I didn't," she says. "But it was kind of like when he was hitting me, it made me feel like, 'At least he loves me, because he wouldn't do this unless he cared.' I know that isn't so at all, but if you want to know what was going on in my mind, there it is."

Her children were well aware of what was going on, she says, even the youngest of them.

"He wasn't hitting them at first," she says. "But he just yelled all the time, you know? And to kids, always having that big voice of a man shouting in their ears, telling them how bad they are, that's almost as bad as getting hit.

"He had no sense of humor. I told him once that he never laughed. I said, 'Lee, it's almost like you never been a kid yourself, the way you are with these kids.' And that was too bad. I mean, the kids and me, we'd be watching television sometimes in the

Mary believed that her boyfriend Lee's beatings were an expression of his love for her. She says she thought, "At least he loves me, because he wouldn't do this unless he cared."

afternoon. There would be something funny happening, someone would fall down or something silly, and me and the kids would laugh. I mean, the kids and me, we'd like grown up together, and we had fun sitting around like that.

"And anyway, he'd say, 'Why you laughing at that? There ain't nothing funny about that.' And he'd yell at the kids for laughing, for making noise. He made them be real quiet. I'll tell you, it got to where we'd hear his key in the door, and we'd all get quiet; we wouldn't laugh or nothing. If there was something funny on TV, we'd change it or turn it off."

"HE'D PINCH THEIR HANDS"

As time went on, Mary says, the children became more and more afraid of Lee, and even though she tried to stop him, he began hurting them, too.

"I guess it wasn't just the kids," she admits. "We were all afraid of him. He would hit the kids—especially when I wasn't home. I mean, that was one thing I wouldn't tolerate. He could hit me, and back then I let that go by, but he knew if he went after my kids in front of me, I'd stop him.

"But like I said, he seemed to do that stuff when I wasn't home. He'd throw shoes at them, hit them with the broom handle. He'd punish them all the time over little things that didn't need more than a scolding. And he'd pinch their hands, too, right on the palms. That hurt them like anything. He had big, hard hands, and those kids would cry. They were little, after all. So I'd come in after being at the store or something, and the kids would tell me about it."

When he was particularly angry at the children—there were six now, since Mary and Lee had had two of their own—he took it out on Mary, she says.

"He'd punch me, call me names in front of the kids, slap me around. I'd have marks afterwards, and his mother would even see those. Then she'd get on Lee, telling him not to do that no more. But she couldn't really do anything. I mean, Lee's father used to do her the same way. That's how Lee learned that stuff."

Mary says that although she did think about getting help, the idea of it embarrassed her.

"It's like I would be admitting that I didn't know what I was doing," she says, shrugging. "I'd be saying what a bad man I had, and that was something I wasn't ready to do. At least not then."

A Gun and a Promise

Mary says that her family became aware of what was going on, and it angered her mother as well as her brother Fred.

"Lee would be hitting me, even in front of my mother sometimes," she says quietly. "She was so sad, not being able to do anything. She'd just sit there, shaking her head. And my brother Fred found out, and he was really mad, really mad.

"I am really close to Fred; I really love him. He came over to our place with a gun one time. He was furious at what Lee had been doing to me. I begged Fred not to shoot him. I didn't want any of that to happen. I mean someone would get killed, someone would go to jail. What if one of my kids got hurt at the same time?

"It was crazy. Lee didn't even get excited. He just sat there, saying, 'Man, I ain't ever done nothing to your sister. I ain't hurt her, what's the matter with you?' Fred didn't shoot him, but he told Lee that he better not lay a hand on me again. And I got to admit, that worked, for a while!"

Mary says that after a time the battering resumed, but that she stopped confiding in her mother and brothers.

"I didn't want them to know," she insists. "Especially Fred, because he'd come over and there would be fighting. I didn't want any of my brothers getting hurt, and they might have. It just seemed like I should figure this all out on my own, anyway."

When the Money Ran Out

Financial worries seemed to increase the violence at home. The government found out that Mary and her children were living with Lee and promptly cut off one of her public aid checks.

"We'd been doing good financially up till then," she says. "I had a part-time job at McDonald's. Lee was working two jobs. Things were okay moneywise. But then after we lost that one welfare check, he lost one of his jobs. Things got tight, and tempers were short. Both of us started drinking. Lee had been drinking all along, but he was into it real heavy now. We'd drink, and then we'd fight—usually about money. We were paying six hundred dollars a month rent, and we were hardly getting by.

"My kids knew what was going on. I mean, we were loud when we were yelling. And of course, Lee would start hitting me, and they saw all of that. They'd run and hide, the little ones. My oldest ones were braver. After Lee would beat me up and leave,

During a calm in their stormy relationship, Lee asked Mary to marry him and she accepted. The night before the ceremony he beat her up, but she went through with the wedding anyway.

they'd come out of their room with some stick or something, and they'd try to be protecting me.

"They'd say, 'Mama, if he comes in here one more time, we're going to hit him with these sticks. We going to bust him upside the head for doing that to you, okay?' But I didn't want them provoking him more, you know what I'm saying? He was already mean, and I didn't want him going after them any more than he was already.

"I know those kids thought I was being mean when I told them to put that stuff down, but I was trying to protect them. If they'd hit him or even tried to go after him with a little stick or something, no telling what he would have done to them. And I figured once we got our finances back in order, things would calm down again. Life might not be perfect, but it'd be better than it was at that time. I knew we couldn't take much more of that."

A WEDDING

As had happened in the past, the violence *did* seem to gradually disappear for awhile, for no apparent reason. For a few months things seemed much calmer between Mary and Lee. His outbursts were fewer, and when they occurred, they involved only words, not violence. It was at this time, says Mary with more than a hint of embarrassment, that she agreed to marry him.

"It sounds real stupid now," she admits, "but I still had these ideas that things were going to be working out better. It was right before Maurice was born. He's my youngest child. We'd been having our good times, and we got talking about it with his mother, thinking about how it would be. I guess I let myself get caught up in all the excitement. I mean, we'd been going months without even a cross word, you know?

"Besides, I had two kids with him and a third on the way. I'll admit, I was still real scared of him. But in a way I was kind of scared not to marry him. It's all jumbled in my mind, but at the time, it seemed like it would be better. And I'd never been married before. The idea of a wedding seemed romantic, with our friends around, everybody dressed up. I know I let all that block out the reality, you know? But we went ahead with the plans.

"The night before we got married, though, he jumped on me, was real rough, and he hit me. The next day I wasn't bruised, but my mama knew. She was so mad at me for going through with that wedding."

AN ACCUSATION

As Mary says, she could have predicted that marriage would not stop the abuse that was becoming a constant threat. Only now, besides physical abuse, there were worries that Lee had been molesting her oldest daughter, an idea that still confuses Mary.

"She didn't say a thing to me at the time," Mary says sadly. "Demetria went through a wild phase, and she would storm out of the house for no reason, it seemed like. I figured she was just emotional, having trouble with her friends or something like that. Lee would be making comments about how she's meeting some boy or other and getting into bad trouble.

"He'd say 'She's probably out doing this,' or 'She's probably out doing that.' See, he wasn't a good father, even when he wasn't beating me. He just didn't remember what it felt like to be a kid. He was always assuming the worst, thinking bad of the kids.

"Well, Demetria started running away. She even ran away to Minnesota to see her real father, but she came back. One time she ended up in a juvenile home. Well, what she said later is that Lee had been messing with her when she was younger, you know, and she was angry about that. She said he'd been touching her, not having sex or nothing, but feeling her, rubbing her."

Mary works in the kitchen while her children eat dinner. Mary and Lee had three children together, but Mary says Lee was a bad father.

Mary said that when her daughter confided in her about that, she confronted her husband. However, in talking with Lee, Mary had doubts about whether it happened.

"I know to this day she is angry at me still, even though we get along," says Mary. "I think she feels I let her down. But honestly, when I asked Lee about it, about his touching her, he seemed cool and calm. He didn't protest, didn't try to defend himself, like he would if he was guilty. I know he'd jump *me*, you know, force me and everything. But he never seemed like no pervert, so I had my doubts."

"I Gave Him a Warning, and I Meant It"

Was there a point at which she knew that the relationship was definitely not going to work? Mary nods.

"I know exactly when things came to a head," she says. "It was about six years that we'd been together. It was the Fourth of July, and a bunch of us were out in the streets having a party right on the corner. We were drinking some beer, having food—you know, just having a holiday get-together with people we knew.

"I was talking to this one friend named Bob. I'd known him a long time before I met Lee. He was a friend, you know, nothing romantic or anything like that. We were laughing and talking— people all around, a whole bunch of us.

"Then Lee came out of nowhere and jumped me in front of all those people. It really hurt me, hurt my feelings, because at that time we'd kind of been getting along. Things had been pretty good. But here he was, smacking me, slapping me. I was standing up against the building, and he hit me so hard I fell down. He was drunk and yelling about how I was a whore and other things that were really dirty.

"I'll tell you, it wasn't so much that this beating hurt any worse than the others. I guess I'd been hit all sorts of ways, and some were probably more painful than that one. He hit me hard once when we were at a gas station. I was pregnant, and I fell down. But on that Fourth of July, boy, that was really bad. It was embarrassing, having everybody standing there watching. It was like I was this dog or something, getting a whupping for doing nothing, and everybody was looking on."

Mary says that no one came to her rescue, most likely because Lee was so out of control.

"Some of them were saying things like, 'Oh, man,' stuff like that. But no one came over and tried to stop him or to help me. I was hurt, I was sad, and I was really embarrassed, like I said.

"When we went back upstairs, I gave him a warning, and I meant it. I told him that if he ever put his hands on me again, I was going to leave him. And I did mean it; I was serious. I think when I was talking to him, telling him that, he really believed me, at least for a time. Now, I'm not going to say that that was the end, or nothing like that. We had fights after that, and things got bad. But they never got *as* bad. And me, I kind of had a feeling that I had a little power there, if I could just use it right, you know?"

ANOTHER WOMAN

Mary says that she got a little more courageous soon afterwards, when it appeared that Lee was seeing another woman.

"The kids knew about it before I did," she says, "because he'd always take them over there when he was supposed to be watching them. He made them swear not to tell me nothing about it, though. How I found out about it was she came under our window and was calling him.

"I was pregnant, had just gotten my public aid check that day, and me and the kids had gone out grocery shopping. Here was this woman, calling, 'Euclid! Euclid!' (His first name was Euclid, but I always called him Lee, his middle name.) But he didn't answer her—I don't even know if he heard her—and she walked away.

"I didn't know what was going on. I really didn't think about it too much, but then he went outside a little bit later. I figured he was going out to sit in his van, like he did sometimes. He had drinking buddies that he met outside all the time. He told me he'd be back. And I watched him out the window, just wondering. I got suspicious, watching. He went to a corner store, and he called me from there. But she was there too, and he didn't know I seen them.

"I said, 'Hey Lee, who's that you're with? She looked to me like she was outside waiting on you. Is that your woman?' He denied it, and so I got mad and hung up on him. And do you think he ever called me back? No."

Mary says that she felt a little guilty later, thinking maybe she had been hasty in her accusations. She went outside, hoping to find Lee with his friends in the van. Lee was there; however, he was definitely not alone.

"There was this girl, sitting right beside him, legs crossed," she remembers. "I walked right up to the van. The girl looked right at me, but Lee just put his head down and kept it there. He knew he'd been caught, and good. The girl said, 'I think I better go,' but I told her no, she didn't have to. I just walked away."

Interestingly, Lee's taking up with another woman was just the spark Mary needed to take her children and leave.

"That Was Courage!"

Mary says she was so angry she could hardly speak. She went back upstairs, told her children to pack their things, and they left, renting a small apartment near her mother-in-law's house.

Little by little, Mary gathered up the strength to leave Lee. Part of her strategy was to call the police whenever Lee would beat her or the kids.

"We were rid of him for two weeks," she says, smiling. "It took that long before he heard from somebody where we were. He came begging back, saying there wasn't nothing between him and that girl. I was at the point where I didn't care, you know? I took him back, but after that, it was like I had more courage, just like after that business after the Fourth of July. It came little by little, but being able to leave him, even for a little while, that was courage!

"I got me a strategy after that. I'd start really calling the police on him whenever he beat me or hurt the kids. I'd have to wait until after the beating, because when he was drunk and angry like that, he was so mean he wouldn't let me near that phone. But when it was over, I'd call, and the police would come.

"Oh, he'd go to jail; they'd take him in," she says. "It wasn't for long—a day or so. He'd go to court, and then he'd come home. They'd always find him, even when he took off after the beating. It got to where sometimes he'd finish hitting me and then just sit on the couch and wait for the police to come get him. He knew he couldn't get away."

Mary says that she was worried at first that Lee would come home from jail angry with her, but that was not the case.

"That man hated jail, and he hated the police," she said. "And the thing is, he knew he done wrong, beating me. He knew he was going to end up in jail. The thing was that he just didn't know it until after he settled down."

FIGHTING BACK

It was a small step from Mary's calling the police on her husband to working up the courage to fight back when he'd begin battering her. It is precisely this fighting back that led to her getting brave enough to leave him—for good.

"I did fight back," she says with a proud grin. "And I ain't saying that violence is good, because I don't think that. But I feel like this kind of man like Lee was, he don't listen to anything else. That's his *way*, you know? He wasn't going to no anger management classes or serving no jail time. Nothing was going to change with him, so I had to do the changing.

"Let me tell you something. Men like him are cowards in a way. They beat you up, long as they think you're afraid. But the first time you pick up something and hit *them*, they're so surprised that they don't know what to expect next.

"Like all this garbage about accusing me of being unfaithful to him with his friends, worrying about me talking to them. Now, he wouldn't go ask his friend if he was doing that, would he? No, he wouldn't bother doing that. He'd go accuse *me*, beat *me* up, because he can whup me, and he might not be able to whup his friend, you see?

"So I'd throw things at him—shoes and things like that. I'd scream and holler as loud as him and threaten to do this or that to him. I stopped sleeping in the same room with him. Me and the kids went into the other room and stayed there. I'd throw hot coffee in his face, and I even picked up his gun and pointed it at him. Yeah, I pulled the trigger, which I'm sorry to this day that I did, but all I did was put a hole in the refrigerator. But I was mad, and if that was the only way to make him back off me, I guess I'd do it."

GETTING OUT

And in the end, Mary says proudly, she and her children simply packed up their things, and announced they were leaving.

"I had found an apartment right next door to my brother Fred. I paid my deposit, and I left. In fact, Lee helped us move! He had no choice. He knew I wasn't taking it no more, and he didn't know what to expect from me next. I wasn't sleeping with him no more, and I told him I didn't want to be with him—ever.

"To be truthful, I wanted him to move, and me and the kids would take the house. After all, it was my check that was paying for the rent. But he didn't want to go. And in the end it was okay, because, like I said, it was nice living right next door to my brother. Lee knew there was nothing in the world he could do about it."

Mary flashes a bright smile.

"See what I mean about standing up for myself?" she says. "It worked!"

It was a matter of weeks before Lee was forced to move from his house. Since he was no longer working, and what money he did have he used for drinking, he was not able to afford the rent that Mary had always paid.

"He came over to my place once in a while," she says, "just to wash up or take a bath. And I'll tell you, he tried to start a little

Although Mary still wishes things had worked out with Lee, she now realizes that she wasn't responsible for Lee's abusive behavior.

trouble sometimes, especially if I was talking to a guy I'd met. Lee would come over and stand by the curb, just looking as jealous as can be, with his arms crossed in front of his chest, you know? I got to admit, I was a little scared, since I'd seen that so many times before, and a beating always used to follow."

"THE PROBLEM WASN'T ME"

In the time since then Mary has had time to reflect on her relationship with Lee. She candidly admits that she wishes things had turned out otherwise with him.

"It's been a while now," she says. "And I'll be real honest—I wish we could have stayed together. I really wish it had worked. I wish Lee had been another way than what he was, you know? I know that I tried harder than I should have but that the problem wasn't me. It was all in him.

"Until I left Chicago, we sort of got along—not as friends or anything, but just not fighting, you know? After all, I had three of his kids, and in his own way he loved them. Not that they could see much of that when we lived together. But after we were apart and they could see that the fighting and hollering had stopped, they got to liking him more. At least they weren't afraid of him no more.

"My older kids have been affected by this, even though he wasn't their father. None of them like him much, never did. And even today they'll get along with him, but only on their terms. If they want to see him for an hour or so, they'll see him. Not Demetria, though; she don't want any part of him.

"If they are around when there's an argument—and I mean *argument*, not fight," she says with a smile, "my older son, Augustus, will get mad, start taking off his shirt like he's going to fight Lee, you know. But Gus, he's a big kid, he's like a man now. He could whup Lee easy. I mean, Lee has been drinking so much for so long, and he's got ulcers and everything . . . he's like an old man, now. He's fifty, but not a healthy fifty, you know what I mean?"

THE YOUNGER KIDS

Mary is confident that her younger kids will be fine, that the violence they experienced back in Chicago will not affect them in negative ways.

"I'll tell you one thing," she says, "my one daughter is having trouble now. She's going through some problems here. She's home from school today because she acted up in class, was smart to her teacher.

"She's thirteen, wants all the kids to like her. But she don't know how. She don't have all the nice clothes, the shoes, whatever, 'cause we don't have the money for that stuff. So she tried to impress them in other ways, like acting up. Only it does the opposite, because none of the kids want to be around her.

"One thing I'm glad about is that her teacher really likes her. She told me she cares a lot for Latrice because she is smart, and the teacher can see that. I'm going to spend some time talking to

Latrice, try to find out what's going on in her head. She had lots of friends back in Chicago, and I think she misses all that."

"I Made Mistakes"

What about the fact that so many children who have lived with an abusive parent grow up to be abusers themselves? Does she ever worry about that?

"I don't think they'd ever grow up to abuse their kids, their wives when they get older," she says, shaking her head. "I was always there for them. I'd talk to them. I raised them mostly myself. He provided for them, but the nurturing was all mine. That's what I did. He never helped, so I don't see much of his influence there. They didn't like what he did to me or what he did to them, so I'd really doubt if they'd grow up to be like him.

"I know I could have done better for them. Don't think I don't know I made mistakes," she says. "I used to get on those kids a lot, hit them and yell when Lee was around, because I didn't want them getting on his nerves. 'Cause you know, he'd whup them worse. And as far as Lee was concerned, he'd get mad at me for letting them off with a scolding. He'd say, 'Why you hollering like that? Why don't you just whup their ass?' And I'd tell him that was no way to deal with kids.

"And when Lee would beat me, I'd be real sad and quiet the next day. I know the kids knew why. They'd come around me saying they wanted to color or play a game or go to the park. But I felt so bad, or sometimes I *looked* so bad, from the beatings, that I'd just tell them to get away from me, leave me alone. They didn't understand why I couldn't get out of my bad mood, I know that now. They probably thought I was being mean to them for no reason, just like Lee was. Sometimes, even now, I feel sorry about that. I think sometimes, I wonder why they still even like me."

"Modest Plans"

Even though her attempts to find a nice apartment for her family have not been successful yet, Mary continues to work at it. In addition, she lines up interviews for part-time jobs, at fast-food places, mostly.

"I have what you might call modest plans," she says. "I mean, I'm thirty-five years old, too old to go back to high school and finish. I know I haven't got the education to get some high-paying job.

102

All of Mary's kids are supposed to give her a helping hand with the cooking.

All I want is to raise my kids in a nice place, work part-time, and be there when they get home from school. I'll work at low-paying jobs, that's fine. I don't need nothing fancy—just to be happy.

"I can make a home out of a little place, and I'm not one to sit and let it get messy. I hate that, always have. I like to keep my place clean. People used to come to my house in Chicago and they couldn't believe it when I told them I have seven kids! My kids know how to help out. They don't expect me to do everything, especially now that they're getting older. They know now to pick up anything that falls on the floor. I don't have to fuss at them much.

"One thing I really like to do is read. It's my favorite thing, really. I been reading everything I can get my hands on around here," she says, pointing to the volume in her lap. "I like mysteries, true stories—I guess anything except love stories. Those things I can't stand! I guess I could write my own love story, only it would get pretty violent, considering what I been through.

"I've read so many books that I forget sometimes and start reading one I'd read a couple years ago. Then I get halfway through it before I realize I remember it. What I'd like to do—part of my plan, anyway—is to join some kind of a book club, where everybody reads the same book, and then we get together and talk about it. That would be cool, yeah. Now I read, and there's nobody to talk about it with. I just start reading another one, then."

"THE SOLUTION WAS IN ME"

Mary shakes her head vehemently when asked if she is seeing any men now.

"I'm not, and I've got no plans to," she says with a grin. "I'm happy, just being with my kids, being on my own. It's nice, espe-

Mary says she doesn't need a man in her life: "I'm happy, just being with my kids, being on my own."

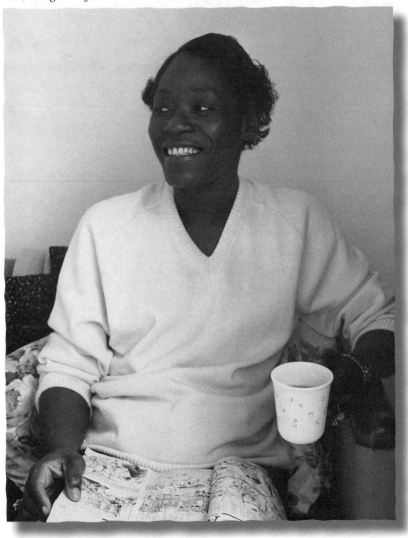

cially when you've been in a relationship where some man's been trying to control your every move, to be in control of yourself finally. I know now that I'll never let anybody take advantage of me ever again. Ever.

"When I met him, I was down and out, you know. And he sort of had that hold on me. But no more. I know I can be without money, but I got hope, and I'm a whole lot smarter than I ever was. All that time, you know, the solution was there. The solution was in me."

Epilogue

In the time since they were first interviewed, the four women whose stories make up *The Other America: Battered Women* have had some interesting changes in their lives.

Megan recently had surgery to remove a cancerous thyroid. She is still waiting to have her stitches removed, but she says the doctors are certain she will recover completely. She has a boyfriend, David, who she says is caring and generous. They have been dating for four months. Although Megan has considered joining the air force, she has put those plans on hold.

Carmen could not be located; a neighbor said she might have taken her children and moved back to Chicago.

Lisa moved into an apartment near one of her girlfriends. Unfortunately, the apartment was infested with roaches, and she had trouble getting her landlord to call an exterminator. She is still seeing her boyfriend, but she is unsure how long the relationship will last.

Mary also moved from the shelter and is living in an apartment in the city. She has no intention of getting involved with anyone soon—and certainly "not with anybody who's going to hurt me or my kids," she says. In addition to the move, Mary has interviewed for a part-time job that will allow her to be home when her children get out of school.

Ways You Can Get Involved

MANY READERS, AFTER FINISHING *THE OTHER AMERICA: BATTERED WOMEN*, MAY BE INTERESTED IN WAYS THEY CAN GET INVOLVED. HERE ARE SOME SUGGESTIONS:

■ Find out what sorts of shelters for battered women exist in your community. Most shelters rely on donations for much, if not all, of their funding; contact one to ask what sorts of supplies they need. You may wish to organize a fund-raiser to benefit the shelter.

■ Shelters often need baby-sitters to watch children when their mothers are attending classes or are looking for more permanent housing. Volunteer to help out a day or two each week.

■ Since you now know that teen girls can be battered women, too, make posters about the problem of dating and violence. Make sure you include phone numbers of support or counseling services that can help girls with these problems.

■ Contact any of the following organizations, who will be glad to send you more information about battered women:

Emerge: A Men's Counseling Service on Domestic Violence
18 Hurley St., Suite 23
Cambridge, MA 02141
(617) 547-9870

Family Service America
11700 West Lake Park Dr.
Milwaukee, WI 53224
(414) 359-1040

**National Coalition Against
Domestic Violence**
PO Box 34103
Washington, DC 20043-4103
(202) 638-6388

**National Council on Child Abuse
and Family Violence**
1155 Connecticut Ave. NW, Suite 300
Washington, DC 20036
(202) 429-6695

For Further Reading

James DeWitt Andrews and Thomas M. Cooey, eds., *William Black-stone, Commentaries on the Laws of England*. Chicago: Callahan, 1891. Invaluable insights into the laws and customs of wife abuse and battering. Excellent notations.

Alisa Del Tufo, *Domestic Violence for Beginners*. New York: Writers and Readers Publishing, 1995. A witty, easy-to-browse-through book, with eye-catching graphics. A good section on the religious and cultural rationalizations given for violence against women.

Donald G. Dutton, *The Batterer: A Psychological Profile*. New York: Basic Books, 1995. Interesting commentary about domestic violence by an expert witness who testified in the O. J. Simpson trial. Interesting information on the family and cultural influences that create men who batter.

Barrie Levy, *In Love and in Danger: A Teen's Guide to Breaking Free of Abusive Relationships*. Seattle, WA: Seal Press, 1993. Very readable handbook for teens who need support in ending a relationship with a battering or otherwise abusive boyfriend. Interesting section explaining the cycle of a batterer.

Claudette McShane, *Warning! Dating May Be Hazardous to Your Health!* Racine, WI: Mother Courage Press, 1988. Very readable book that concentrates on the abuse encountered by teenagers in dating relationships.

Ginny NiCarthy and Sue Davidson, *You Can Be Free: An Easy-to-Read Handbook for Abused Women*. Seattle, WA: Seal Press, 1989. Fascinating step-by-step instructions for battered women, from making the decision to leave to understanding what's involved in checking into a women's shelter.

Index

ABOUT THE AUTHOR

Gail B. Stewart is the author of more than eighty books for children and young adults. She lives in Minneapolis, Minnesota, with her husband, Carl, and their sons, Ted, Elliot, and Flynn. When she is not writing, she spends her time reading, walking, and watching her sons play soccer.

Although she has enjoyed working on each of her books, she says that *The Other America* series has been especially gratifying. "So many of my past books have involved extensive research," she says, "but most of it has been library work—journals, magazines, books. But for these books, the main research has been very human. Spending the day with a little girl who has AIDS, or having lunch in a soup kitchen with a homeless man—these kinds of things give you insight that a library alone just can't match."

Stewart hopes that readers of this series will experience some of the same insights—perhaps even being motivated to use some of the suggestions at the end of each book to become involved with someone of the Other America.

ABOUT THE PHOTOGRAPHER

Twenty-two-year-old Natasha Frost has been a photographer for the *Minnesota Daily*, the University of Minnesota's student newspaper, for three and a half years. She currently attends the University of Minnesota and is studying sociology and journalism.

When not working at the paper or going to school, Frost enjoys traveling. "It gives me a chance to meet different people and expand my knowledge about the world."